ΟΝΕ
PARMENIDES AND HIS VISION

James Cowan

Balgo Hills
Publishing

Copyright © 2022 James Cowan Estate

Written in 2016

All rights reserved.

The author has asserted his right to be identified as the author of this work in accordance with the Copyright, Design and Patents Act 1988.

ISBN-13: 978-1-913816-62-9

First published in this edition: 2022
by Balgo Hills Publishing

Cover & Book Design: Amedée & Benjamin

The One remains, the many change and pass;
Heaven's light forever shines, Earth's shadows fly;
Life, like a dome of many-coloured glass
Stains the white radiance of Eternity...

    Percy Bysshe Shelley

CONTENTS

Introduction	1
Way of Truth	11
Reflections	23
Afterword	163
Appendix	175
Select Bibliography	178
Diagrams Of One	180

Introduction

In the history of western thought there is one man who stands out as a person of unique importance. That man is Parmenides, a philosopher born into a tiny Greek city - state known as Elea in southern Italy in early sixth century BCE. We know little about his life, though we do know that he wrote a poem which changed the way we think. His *Way of Truth* stands like an old oak tree on a hill, its branches extending to the horizon. Parmenides made it possible for our distant forebears to think outside the long - established envelope of myth, that secure haven of people in days past, including many of our beloved epic poets and lyricists. In so doing he pioneered logical thinking, and he used it to construct the science that we know today as metaphysics.

For many years I had thought of Parmenides as a remote figure in the history of philosophy, someone who was unapproachable. As I grew disenchanted with modernity and the collapse of any sense that absolutes might exist, I increaseingly found myself returning to his monumental poem for guidance. I call it 'monumental' not because it is a long poem, but because it says something about the existence of a fundamental truth lying at the very heart of our understanding of the universe. I began to see that Parmenides wanted to draw a line in the sand that others such as myself might venture to cross: his ambition was to do nothing less than encourage me to think as a fully rounded person, a whole man, about the nature of the mystery into which we are born.

At first, I did not know how to enter his poem. It struck me as opaque, utterly confusing, and filled with utterances more in keeping with a half-crazed sibyl than a serious philosopher. But I did not give up on him. Year after year, whenever I was feeling a little down or confused, I returned to his poem and allowed it to interrogate me. Who was I? What was I doing with my life? Did I have a destiny? These were the sort of questions that filled my thoughts as I tried to come to terms with Parmenides' relentless and sometimes unyielding logic. He was testing me. At the same time he made me feel inadequate, even shallow, one of those people the Aborigines of Australia call an *inapertwa*, a rudimentary or half-man. It occurred to me that whenever I was in his presence I had no place to hide.

Eventually I had to tell myself that Parmenides was no ordinary thinker. To write such a poem he must have been truly inspired. He must have encountered a god or goddess who cared for him. Yes, cared, I told myself. He had put his trust in the fact that he was not alone in the world, that nature was not to be feared, and that his presence as a thinking, self-aware person contributed to the deification of matter itself. Until I read Parmenides' poem I had never thought about the everyday world living its own interior life, untouched by my observations or demands. I had always seen it as inert, devoid of purpose, very much a formless entity to be manipulated by myself and others, each according to our own self-interest.

Parmenides taught me the error of my ways. It took a long time, many years in fact, before I began to understand that I was looking at life through a haze created by the various illusions of my time. It possessed no clarity of thought. I was simply a person reacting from one day to the next without thought of the consequences of my problematic and sometimes unthinking nature. This, Parmenides told me, was because I saw the world one-dimensionally, as I might when peering through a telescope. The clarities that I thought were there to see may have been magnified, but they were utterly false. I had replaced his simple sense of oneness with the dubious delights of multiplicity and diversion, then very much a part of the life I led.

In this book I trace my encounter with Parmenides, the poet as much as the philosopher. It is not an academic study, but an attempt to bring the philosopher back to life as a real presence in our modern age. I wanted to see him as an inspired poet before I regarded him as one of the seminal thinkers belonging to the western canon. As a poet, he struggled with words and with images all his life. Any difficulties one finds in his poem are there because he was attempting to create a new language, the language of pure metaphysics. Those who came after him, men such as Zeno, Empedocles, Socrates, Plato, Plotinus and Proclus, were indebted to his pioneering work. He showed them that it was possible to write inspired verses that gave life meaning - and, more importantly, which presented them with the logic of an absolute with which to grapple as a philosophic premise and aid to dealing with life.

Scholars over the past century have mined the *Way of Truth* for every philological nugget that they could possibly unearth. They have translated the poem with careful attention to its literal meaning. They have considered its style as one beholden to Homer and even Hesiod. Burying the poem under a mountain of commentary as they have done has allowed these scholars to sometimes forget that the *Way of Truth* is, firstly, a work of art and not a tome. It is not a treatise, either. As a result, Parmenides has been shunted to one side as little more than a follower of Heraclitus or a precursor to Plato and later philosophers such as Aristotle and Plotinus. Few saw him as a visionary whose words would never lose their universality or their glister, in spite of how they might have interpreted him.

Before I decided to write this book, I knew that I must first address the poem as a work of art. If the *Way of Truth* was to sing again, then it had to be rescued from the commentary under which it had lain for so long. It meant approaching Parmenides' verses as an inspired poet and not as a scholar. Thankfully a well - known poet from last century came to my rescue, someone who enabled me to piece together my thoughts about his poem.

His name was Ezra Pound, an early American modernist, who had himself rendered an obscure medieval poem called *The Seafarer* into modern verse. By careful use of his craft as a poet, Pound brought back to life this Old English poem so that we might enjoy its beauty and universality today. Pound's dictum in those days, back in 1911 when he lived as a young poet in London, was to 'make it new'. The remark was said to have been inscribed on a washbasin of the first king of the Shang Dynasty in China (1766-1753 BCE). Like Pound, I made this maxim my template for rewriting Parmenides' great poem for a modern audience. I wanted to make it new again.

I do not claim that my rendition is an exact translation of either the ancient Greek text or the more scholarly prose renditions that we possess, such as those by Professors John Burnet, F.M Cornford, W.C.K. Guthrie, and E.R. Dodds. Instead I have returned to the spirit of the poem itself, rather than to attempt a careful literal translation. I wanted my rendition of Parmenides' verses to sing in the way that they must have done for its hearers in Elea, Acragas, and Athens at the turn of the sixth - century BCE, when rhapsodists uttered its verses for the first time. Socrates remarked favorably on the poem when he heard it in Athens as a young man, so Plato tells us in his dialogue, *Parmenides*. He was in awe at the richness and profundity of its verses. Over the centuries since then philosophers from Plato to Nietzsche have been greatly influenced by the poem.

This book is an account of a journey I decided to make into an almost forgotten Pre - socratic poem. I encountered many byways along the road. But what I finally discovered was a poem as pure as any that has been written. The *Way of Truth* has managed to survive the wreckage of Greek culture following the rise of Rome and the subsequent advent of Christianity throughout the Mediterranean world, and gone on to become a beacon of wisdom for us all. I believe it still has something to say, as its message lies at the very bedrock of western civilization. What Parmenides says to us is part of our cultural and spiritual legacy. In one short poem he has shown us how to live our lives in the spirit of freedom and fearlessness.

In the following pages I offer my reflections on his groundbreaking poem, the *Way of Truth*. Its verses are diamond - hard. One can try and break them open, but they will resist. This is because they are made up of something that transcends matter itself. They have come into existence as a result of one extraordinary man, Parmenides, who chose to explore his own path of truth as a part of his commitment to understanding the mystery of life. In fact, understanding the miracle of the entire universe! He sought to hear within himself echoes of the world's symphony, and to translate these into poetic concepts for us all.

Read it at your pleasure. Hopefully it will change you as it did me.

A Brief History of the Poem

Parmenides' poem has come down to us as a series of fragments only. We do not have a complete copy as it was written; but rather, we possess verses and stanzas unearthed from the writings of others, in particular Simplicius who supplied us with fifty - three lines. The *Way of Truth* is much like an archeological site: we see the outline of a temple on the ground, a few pillars rising into the air, and the remains of empty benches in a circus or gymnasium. The poem has been put together by many thoughtful scholars over the millennia, each working within the limitation of their knowledge and capacities. So that, inevitably, we find ourselves gazing as though through a cloudy piece of glass at words obscured by time and loss.

Many early writers have contributed to our knowledge of the poem, not least men such as Diogenes Laertius, Sextus Empiricus, Simplicius, Aristotle, Proclus, Plotinus, Plato, Clement, Plutarch, Strobaeus, and Theophrastus. These ancient scholars have all helped us to put together what Parmenides originally wrote. It must be remembered, though we do not know for certain, that the poem was likely translated from old Ionic into Attic Greek along the way, so that aspects of its original fluency may have been lost. Opinion is divided over exactly how much of the poem we possess. Some suggest that we possess perhaps ninety percent of the *Prologue* and the *Way of Truth;* others, that we only have less than ten percent of the *Way of Appearance*. All of which tells us that we are dealing with a fragmentary poem much affected by interpolation and time.

We do know, however, that subsequent philosophers and commentators valued enormously what Parmenides had written. He informed their many books to the extent that his belief in concepts such as One, Being, being and the illusion of appearance, were fundamental to understanding how they viewed reality. A mighty insight had landed in their midst, and it took several hundred years for them to absorb and understand his message.

Finally all these fragments that we have were gathered together in the modern era by two German scholars, Alexander Deils and Walther Kranze, who translated and ordered the text we use today in their book, *Fragments of the Presocratics* (1903). It is thanks to their patient scholarship that future generations have been allowed to enter Parmenides' great poem.

The *Way of Truth* is a very ancient, important, but incomplete document written by a philosophic genius. As you begin to read it, think of yourself as picking up an abandoned piece of ostraca lying on the ground in some ruin, revealing as it does a few, barely legible Greek letters inscribed upon its surface. Before you, let it be imagined, are some hints and allusions of great import from a distant past. These will introduce you to a rarified world, the world of Parmenides and his unique concept of One.

Way of Truth

The poem

PROLOGUE

A chariot bore me as far as my heart desired
Urging me upon the Way of the Goddess
That leads wise men from town to town.
On that Way I was hauled by trusty steeds
Hitched to a chariot, & driven by maidens.
Its axle glowed fiery red in their hubs, heated by
Spinning wheels at each end, both emitting sounds
Of a panpipe, while the Daughters of the Sun
Wishing to transport me into the light, tossed aside
Veils from their faces as we left Night's abode.

Before me were the gates between Night & Light
Above a lintel, a threshold of stone below.
Huge doors rose high in the air, their keys
In the hands of stern Justice. My maidens
Pleaded with her using gentle words, hoping
To persuade the Goddess to unlock the giant bolts
On these cloud-lined gates. And they opened
Slowly, one after the other, on bronze posts
Covered with cast-iron rivets & nails, to reveal

A broad & unending expanse beyond.
Through them we passed on a wide avenue
Under the whip of my guides, horses galloping
Chariot rumbling as we approached the Goddess.
She greeted me kindly, and took my right hand
In hers, before uttering these undying words:

Welcome, young man, you who come to my abode
On a chariot driven by immortal maidens!
It's no ill luck but Truth and Justice who urged you
To travel on this Way. It lies a great distance
From the beaten track of ordinary men.
You must now learn many new things, &
Crack open the shell of truth well concealed
So that men's opinions might best be understood
As no true belief at all. You will learn
Fresh things also – that, by embracing them
You will discover how illusory some are, others
Fortified by the pure actuality of thought.

Don't be afraid from engaging in inquiry
Nor let familiarity blind your gaze
As the voice of gossip by tongue or ear;
Listen to well argued proofs uttered by me.
Only one Way can be fruitfully discussed.

The Way of Truth

With the aid of your thoughts look seriously
At distant forms, as if they were close at hand.
Never sever *what is* from remaining true
To *what is*. Resist allowing it to be scattered
Abroad as its opposite, *what isn't*. Illusory
Is the nature of being when widely dispersed.

Where I begin is all One to me, & I will
Return again & again to this refrain.

Listen, & I will tell you – what I say must
Be stored in your mind, & never forgotten:
Apprehending & being are one & the same.
It is can never be confused with not-being
For such is Truth, your constant companion.
What *is not* can never be, not now
Or in the future, however much you might
Wander down various pathways, hoping
To distance yourself from the unity of One.
Remember, what *is not* cannot be known
Nor can it be properly uttered, impossible!

It's a contradiction, a two-headed beast
Befuddling a confused mind, amazing everyone
For whom being & not-being are thought of
As the same, an entrance to a blind alley.

Try to prevent yourself travelling along
This barren road; know that what can be
Spoken about and thought of *is*, rather
Than nothing, that bland celebration of
The simple properties of existence. This
Is what you must think about before you
Wander afar spouting everyday opinions
To all & sundry, as if the contingent was real.
The average person believes that what *is*
& what *is not* are real distinctions, when
They're no more than flotsam on a beach.

Impossible to prove – things that aren't *are*
When they clearly partake of falsity. Don't
Even think about it when you consider
Which fork in the road you need to take.

There's only one path to reconoitre, namely
That *it is*. On this there are signs aplenty
To indicate that Being is indestructible
Ungenerated, of a wholeness, immovable
& without end. Nor *was* it ever, nor *will*
It be, since it's always & forever *is*.
What beginning are you looking for, what

Origin, what source that might suggest
That it can *grow*? I'll not allow
You to apprehend it emerging from what *is not*.
If it's not sayable or thinkable, then surely
It must remain in the domain of falsity only.
And what need would have impelled it
Then or later, to finally *grow*, if its
Origin lies in no thing? Either it must *be*
In wholeness or not at all! Nor will
Truth's ardor allow anything to compete
With its being, least of all what *is not*.
Justice simply refuses to release its hold
Upon things, so that they might pass away
Or come into being. Not at all! A decision
In these matters lies in *it is* or… *it is not*.

It is has been decided, and the other path
Of not-being but a nameless chimera
That leads nowhere, rocky & uncertain.
The true path leads to the imperishable nature
Of what *is*, unbecoming, a beacon that defies
The darkness of not-being, since it never
Came to be in the first place! to die
Or be born are questions that can't be asked.

Nor can it be divided, since it's all of a likeness.
There's no more of it in one place than another
To prevent it from holding together.
Nor less of it, embodying fullness of what *is*

As it does, an ongoing cohesive whole
Drawn by itself into One that is of itself,
An empty bolus of unmitigated essence.

Mighty chains bind it to its unbeginning
& to its unceasing, since birth and death
Have been driven to a far place by Truth
& so banished as states that can't exist.
Always it's the same, & rests in its sameness
Alone, a constant, at the mercy of Necessity
Hemming it tightly within the bonds of Limit.
Nor is it able to partake of the infinite, of
The incomplete, as it is in need of nothing,
Forever existing as it does, without lack.
A thing thought, & what promotes that thought, *is*.
Without what *is*, & its utterance, there can be
No thought, not even a whimsy. Nothing *is*
Or ever will be in the wake of being, enchained
As it is by Destiny to wholeness & a pure state
Of the inert. All things are no more than names
We attribute as truthful – coming into being
Or perishing, being & not being, even
Changing from one place to another.
Bright colours merging into dullness
Is little more than a perception, unreal.

One is empowered by Limit, complete
On all sides, like the content of a sphere
Rounded, equipoised, neither large nor small

Reacting in all directions equally, inviolate
Perfectly attuned to uniform within Limit.

At this point I cease my argument about
Thought & speech as the essence of Truth
& I ask you to listen to how deceitful I can be
When it comes to arranging my words.

The Way of Appearance

Two concepts men have chosen to announce
Of which one should never have been named
Because it leads away from Truth. Opposing
One concept over another as a *distinction*
Has lead to the light of dawn in all its softness
Being contrasted to darkness as a compact
Heavy mass. This is appearance only, which
You accept so that you are not deceived.

But it's false, because what seems to be
Can never overshadow the claims of Truth
Given that all things share light & darkness
Equally, one as real as the next.

Know that the sky, with all its signs, including
The pure flame of the sun, is a familiar sight.

Do you not learn to recognize the moon's nightly
Peregrinations, its round face & sly crescents
What it is made of? Of course! The Goddess
Necessity binds them together, the earth
Stars, moon & sky, the Milky Way & Olympus'
Grave slopes, are all one resplendent whole,
A part of the sphere's foundation & limit.
Unmixed fire's slender rings proximate
To night offers up its portion of light, yet
Can't dispense with iron's configuration
Or the miracle of the moon. These are
Needful of the sun's rays, since Necessity
Directs their heavenly course with the wand
Of Love & birth's labour, expressed as it is
By the embrace of man & woman, Eros
Her first-born in the unending firmament.

Shining by night with borrowed light
Does the moon wander about the earth
Always indebted to the sun's rays.
Just as thought blends with men's misbehaving
Limbs, know that it is the *whole body* thinking
In every one of us, since thought is regal
The very substance of all our mortal coils.
Depending on how much light or darkness exists
In our bodies, so do we embody wisdom
Or its foolish opponent, cretinous opinion.

On the right males, females on the left…

When man & woman blend their love-seed
An energy is unleashed in the body as blood
Intermingles & becomes one. If this power
Is right then strong, well - built bodies result.
If wrong, if the power of one blood fights
For supremacy, trouble will arise. It's not
Right for someone to be born from twin seeds.

Mark well, all this is merely opinion
That formulates & grows, then fades away
As mature thought intervenes. And yet
At some point each was given a name
As if it partook of the very bliss of being.

REFLECTIONS

I

I have lived in the company of the ancient Greek philosopher known as Parmenides for more than thirty-five years, ever since I had first read his poem, the *Way of Truth*. At the beginning of our encounter I confess I hardly understood a word of what he was trying to say. The poem reminded me of the most perfectly conceived abstraction, so *koan* - like were its enigmatic utterances and rejoinders. How could a man think the way he did? What was he trying to say? It was as if I had wandered into a vast cavern filled with stalactites all channeling their calcinated essence from some remote and inaccessible roof. If I were a speleologist, then my first foray into the cavern of his mind yielded no more than a fragmented array of thought - images that had no bearing on reality.

Or so I thought.

Over the years I picked up the poem and resumed my engagement. Normally I would have lost interest in such a work if I had only considered it to be 'just another poem'. It stumped me, however. It made me feel inadequate. I kept asking myself whether I lacked some fundamental capacity to decipher its message. Was there something in my makeup that made it impossible to comprehend the journey he was asking me to make? Was I *afraid* of where it might lead? At this point I would put aside the poem and retreat into what I already knew. Life, with its unceasing demands, seemed to be more pressing than the task of plumbing the depths of a 2,500 year old poem. I told myself that it was no more than a 'fragment' anyway, that its real meaning lay elsewhere – lost, no doubt, beneath the accumulated debris of time.

But the poem would not let me go so easily. Parmenides haunted my thoughts on and off over the ensuing years. I kept going back to the poem, reading different translations and commentaries about its structure and history, pondering its meaning. In the process I found myself slowly becoming displaced: the poem had taken on the semblance of a shadow-play, its obscure configurations taunting me with their gestures and arguments, much as if they were reflected upon a screen. I was in the hands of a master puppeteer, someone who delighted in wielding power over my thoughts by way of his austere and unrelenting rigor. Here was a man who had become fully *present* in my life; he had quit his eyrie on the rocky promontory of the past and flown down to meet me.

This is the way of all great minds, I told myself. They captivate us with the loftiness of their meditations. How could I not acknowledge that Parmenides had begun the difficult task of lifting me out of myself, so that I might think differently to the way I had been trained? That is a major call: to think differently, to apply one's mind in such a way that allows one to experience an enhanced vision of the world, is certainly some achievement. Parmenides was no ordinary philosopher in the mold of Pythagoras or Plato. Unlike these philosophers his personality did not reveal itself so easily. He did not prefer to eat beans or live the simple life, nor did he suggest that he wanted to found an academy or gather followers to his cause. Rather, he was a man who at some point in his life experienced the full force of a revelation too important not to offer it up to the world.

   I cast about among other philosophers and poets who had changed the way I thought in the past. Over a lifetime there had been many who have made me view the world in a new and refreshing way. I kept telling myself that a knowledge of beauty and clarity of reasoning are not accidently acquired, but come about as a result of a long engagement with what constitutes their essence. One must learn how to perceive beauty; one has to learn how to think in an untrammelled way free of all prejudice or the cliché of opinion.

   Visionaries are not normal people; their entire mental approach is determined by the realization that they have to break out of the carapace of their daily existence if they are ever to bring forth something new. Their modus is that of a cicada: they live deep in the soil of their thoughts until the moment when they need to climb up and out of themselves. It is at this moment when they offer us new insight, and provide us with the exhilaration of reading or hearing an original poem for the very first time.

Parmenides inhabits such a terrain. He lived at a time when people were fleeing the Persians in Phocaea in western Asia Minor. War and rupture were ever present. His family were not the first to quit either the island of Samos or the city of Miletus nearby in their bid to find a safer place to live. Pythagoras had done so years earlier, fleeing the tyrant Polycrates. He had sailed to Croton in Magna Graecia (southern Italy) around 530 BCE, after many years in Egypt in the company of priests of the temple at Heliopolis. There he later founded his philosophic community based upon what he had learnt from them.[1] We know little of Parmenides' background other than he was born into an important family in his home town of Elea (ie. Hyele, also known today as Velia), in southern Italy around 515 BCE. At least according to Plato, who tells us that his teacher Socrates met the philosopher

· · · · · · · · · · · · ·

[1] See Plutarch, *Isis and Osiris*. 'Witness to this also are the wisest of the Greeks: Solon, Thales, Plato, Eudoxus, Pythagoras, who came to Egypt and consorted with the priests; and in this number some would include Lycurgus also. Eudoxus, they say, received instruction from Chonuphis of Memphis, Solon from Sonchis of Saïs, and Pythagoras from Oenuphis of Heliopolis. Pythagoras, it seems, was greatly admired, and he also greatly admired the Egyptian priests, and, copying their symbolism and occult teachings, incorporated his doctrines in enigmas. As a matter of fact most of the Pythagorean precepts do not at all fall short of the writings that are called hieroglyphs.'

as a young man, when he came to Athens to attend the Panathenaic Games.

Magna Graecia was part of the New World of the Greek diaspora at that time, exciting to many, a challenge to others. It was incumbent upon the old families from Phocaea when they arrived to bring their culture, their gods and cult statures, as well as their philosophic inclination, to this new land, if they were ever to transplant themselves successfully. Elea was no Wild West of its time, as many might believe, but a centre for a people long habituated to the Greek ideal from earlier migrations.

According to Herodotus, we are told that the city was founded on the advice of the Pythian Oracle dedicated to Apollo in Delphi, after the Phocaeans had sailed away from their old homeland to Corsica where they had originally landed.[2] She informed their representative, who had gone to Delhi seeking her advice about where to go next, that his people needed to listen to a certain 'man from Posedonia' a stranger no less, who later directed them to found their city not far from his own in southern Italy. That was after their attempt to found a colony on Corsica had failed. All of that region of southern Italy was then considered to be the mythical land of Hercules. The land around Elea itself was dedicated to the hero's son, Cyrnus.

- - - - - - - - - - - - -
2   Herodotus, *Histories*. Bk I.167

Parmenides grew up in a town steeped in heroic memory. The 'stranger from Posidonia' was probably one of those wise men that wandered throughout southern Italy during those times, many of them old Pythagoreans who had left Croton or Metapontum where the Master had met his untimely death.[3] Such men were members of loosely knit religious societies known as *thiasoi*, as distinct from those who were members of political societies known as *hetaireiai*. A city needed a hero to affirm its existence, and the stranger had presented himself as one to them – and at the right time for these displaced Phocaeans eager to find a new homeland.

Parmenides' father's name was Pyres. He taught him to be a good and upright citizen. He was later repaid for his efforts when his son helped to frame the laws of their newly founded city, and possible became one of its archons. One must assume that the young Parmenides lived a normal life closely attached to the soil, even if he was not a farmer himself. Elea occupied high ground near the Tyrrhenian Sea, its knoll possessing the ruins of an amphitheatre to this day. We cannot be sure that the theatre existed in Parmenides' time, but we must assume that a yearning to recreate a cultural environment that mirrored that of their Melesian homeland was acute. Books and ideas are easily transported; the construction of edifices require time and a more settled existence.

∙∙∙∙∙∙∙∙∙∙∙∙∙

3   See Iamblichus, *Life of Pythagoras*. 'It happened that all Italy was filled with philosophers, and this place, which before was unknown, was afterwards on account of Pythagoras, called Magna Graecia.'

Parmenides was born into a society firmly committed to the cultivation of civic values and the delights of thought.

Why do I say this? Firstly, I can't see Parmenides springing forth from virgin ground. His genius had to be nurtured by something – or someone. Diogenes Laertius tells us that his teacher was a man named Ameinias, the son of Diochaetas, said to be one of those itinerant philosophers mentioned earlier, and possibly a friend of the Master.[4] Iamblichus also names Parmenides as a Pythagorean, the only one from Elea.[5] His early years of majority were spent in the company of a man who reached back to the great Pythagoras himself.

Moreover, he had entered into a tradition of knowledge handed down from one sage to another, as was the practice in those days through the *thiasos* societies. Parmenides would have likely learnt about the mathematical structure of reality, about harmony, metempsychosis, as well as other secret teachings espoused by the Master when he was alive, from this 'worthy gentleman', so

---

4   Diogenes Laertius, *Lives of the Eminent Philosophers.* Bk. IX, ch.3.

5   Ibid. Iambl. *Life.* Nor did Iamblichus mention the philosophers Xenophanes or Zeno, colleagues of Parmenides, who lived in Elea for many years. Xenophanes wrote a poem about the history of the city. One must assume that Parmenides tested his ideas on his friend, before he wrote his own poem. This list, however, has been contested as a pan-Pythagorean fabrication to justify the perceived extent of Pythagoreanism in Italy.

Laertius tells us, 'who happened to be poor'.⁶ Parmenides acquired the discipline of thinking metaphysically from a man, namely Ameinias, who himself had dismissed the accouterments of wealth as being unworthy of the philosophic life. No wonder Parmenides became so attached to him.

According to Laertius, Parmenides was so devoted to Ameinias that he built a shrine to honour him at his death. In doing so, he elevated his teacher to that of a hero of the city *(heros ktistes)*. This was not an uncommon practice in those days, such a merging of the wise man and the hero. We know that Parmenides was also raised to the status of a hero after his death.⁷ In 1962, in Elea, an inscription dedicated to him was unearthed, carved on a broken block of marble. The statue of the philosopher had been set up by the city fathers in honour of one of their favorite sons, even if it was some hundreds of years later. It read: *Parmenides, son of Pyres, Ouliades Physikos*. This was my first clue as to who Parmenides might really have been, at least in the eyes of his contemporaries. He was an *ouliades*, a healer.

• • • • • • • • • • • • • •

6   Ibid. Laert. *Lives*.

7   Plato tells us *(Republic* 427b) that the building of hero shrines was important to the foundation of a city. That both Ameinias and Parmenides were so honoured suggests that the people of Elia were proud of their philosophers. It is also interesting to note that in the history of Elia, Parmenides' death is considered the founding moment from which all subsequent years were counted, as in Christianity from the year when Christ was born.

We are accustomed to think of philosophers as men of learning and intellect, not as those who practice the healing arts. In Greek there are two words that signify a healer. One is *physikos,* a word that might identify a Hippocrates or Asclepius, both doctors in the recognized sense. The other is *ouliades,* which suggests another order of healing to do with that of cultivating the interior life. Parmenides was considered by his fellow Eleatics to be an *ouliades* - that is, a spiritual healer, as well as a lawmaker.[8] He was a man who had undergone some sort of initiation into an ancient order that healed through imparting esoteric knowledge of the good life. Pythagoras was such a man too, as was Ameinias. Both men, so we are told, wandered from town to town at different times in their lives, 'not to teach but to heal'.

Through his long friendship with Ameinias, Parmenides had adopted a Pythagorean worldview. Friendship between an older and a younger man in those days meant much more than it does today. The student surrendered his identity to that of his teacher. Often the older man formally adopted his young friend, thereby assuring that the knowledge he imparted became more familial than fraternal. Adoption had a religious connection to it in that it more than likely alluded to knowledge of the mysteries associated with such cults as those of Orpheus. In this way a young man such as Parmenides

----

8   Healing and justice were often associated when good laws were introduced in order to 'heal' a city. So that as an *ouliades,* Parmenides was very much involved in both inner and outer healing.

could be considered as the 'son of Apollo Oulios', or an *Ouliades*. He was wedded to a god, to Apollo. He was also wedded to the healing arts of the soul.

I was a little nearer to understanding Parmenides and his origins. He was not simply a philosopher; he was something more. He was a man in league with ancient teachings that, though promulgated in Croton by Pythagoras and his followers, nonetheless reached back to the land of his forefathers, to Phocaea in Asia Minor, a land steeped in the worship of Apollo. The tradition from which he emerged was derived from Phocaea itself. And why should this be so important? Because Miletus, its principal city, marked the end of the great trade - route from the East – from Persia, the land of Zoroaster, and more distantly from India.[9] Not only exotic goods arrived from a far place to this thriving entrepot in Ionia, but also – and more importantly – ideas.

Even as I began to understand from where Parmenides had come, I started to realize how essential it is to understand the various cultural connections from which he emerged. Though a man of good family, at some point in his life he found himself entering into a new mode of existence through his friendship with Ameinias. The sage did not teach him how to think so much as how to participate more deeply in Being. Far from learning how to be a logical human being – a discipline that many scholars believe Parmenides invented –

. . . .
9   It is known that there were a number of Indians among Xerxes' army when they invaded Greece. (West: EGP)

his background in Asia Minor helped him to think 'irrationally' at the same time. Through the insights that he received from his teacher he learnt how to think primordially, and so transcend the normal constraints of any irrational - rational dichotomy. Ameinias taught him the most important lesson of all: how to centre himself in Being, as distinct from contemplating it from a distance.

But this is to reach too far ahead in my story. I want Parmenides and his great poem to slowly come to us across the millennia, as it must have for his contemporaries. I am not dealing with an ordinary man or an ordinary poem. Parmenides is no Homer, nor a Pindar. But this fact doesn't make him any less of a poet. Rather, he a poet who has decided to use poetry as his method of coming to terms with a profoundly moving moment in the history of humankind. I know that there are a few such poets as Dante and Shakespeare who make these claims upon us, and rightly so. The *Bhagavad Gita* enthralls us to the extent that we marvel at its worldview. There's a long history of great poets and their poems that we honour for what they say. But there is only one *Way of Truth*.

II

We catch a glimpse of Parmenides as an older man in the pages of Plato's great dialogue, *Parmenides*. Plato tells us that the philosopher arrived in Athens to attend the Panathenaic Games when he was in his sixty - fifth year, in 450 BCE. 'Well advanced in years, with hair almost white', Plato writes, he nonetheless bore a 'distinguished appearance'. Socrates, who was no more than twenty at the time, met him at the home of Antiphon, a member of the philosophic community of Athens. Socrates had gone to Antiphon's house to meet Zeno, Parmenides adopted son and disciple, whom he knew by reputation. He and Zeno were nearer in age, so they would have had more in common. Though Socrates tells us that he admired Zeno, whom he described as 'tall and attractive', his real admiration was directed towards Parmenides who accompanied him. Socrates described him as being 'venerable and awful', possessing 'a glorious depth of mind'.

In the house of Antiphon, on the outskirts of Athens, I meet Parmenides for the first time. It is a meeting I would never have thought possible until I had read Plato's dialogue. Many scholars argue that the meeting simply 'did not happen', that it was a fiction devised by Plato to explore Parmenides' ideas. Be that as it may, I do sense that I have now met the man. The description of him strikes me as real, not some idea of what a philosopher might be expected to look like. He is a venerable old man, a man who has grown into his revelation – a revelation that others knew about, including Socrates and later Plato, since they both acknowledged that they had read or heard the *Way of Truth*, and were familiar with its argument. Socrates goes so far as to suggest that Zeno's treatise, which the latter read to them that day in Antiphon's house, merely echoed what Parmenides had previously written.

To this repost Parmenides vigorously came to the defense of Zeno, his young friend, and one whom he treated as a equal *(kolna ta philon)*, against the suggestion of plagiarism of his own work. 'You are still young, Socrates,' he chided, 'and philosophy has not yet taken hold of you so firmly, as I believe it will some day.' At once I am aware of the rigor of the man's demeanor, and his refusal to be waylaid by a younger man testing his mettle. 'Philosophy has yet to take hold' carries with it an injunction to live inside philosophy as a hermit crab does in its shell. It is not a game but a way of life, a method of attaining to *autarcheia* or inner freedom. As Polemon, one of the heads of the Old Academy in Athens (and a friend of Socrates), remarked, 'We must exercise ourselves with realities, not with dialectical speculations.'[10] Parmenides is saying to Socrates not to engage in an act of sophistry with him or Zeno because they know what they are saying to be true – as well, they say it as one person. Stealing one another's ideas is simply not an issue for either men.

This is the man I have since come to know. Parmenides is no shrinking violet where serious thinking is concerned. He knows that his poem is unbreakable, a glittering gem of thought. If Zeno chooses to celebrate its content in prose rather than in poetry, has it lost any of its gravity for becoming more prosaic? Parmenides has come to Athens, perhaps for the first time in his life, in order to defend his poem from the sophistries of Socratic dialectic. Far from attending the Games as an observer, he is in Athens to counter what is the general disposition by many to make philosophy into a game of the intellect. Even Socrates admitted, that on his first encounter with Parmenides, he recognized a man who was awful, or awe - filled.

The Greeks have a word for awe. That is, *sebastos*. To regard a man as one filled with *sebastos* was to give a person a name proper to the numen, to rank him by the category proper only to the numen. It is a word that we associate with 'dread'. We know that Socrates

---

10 Laertius, Bk. 4, 16-18.

had a reputation for seeing through things and into the heart of certain people, almost as if he was in a trance. Some found this capacity of his engaging; others thought it symptomatic of someone who, in common parlance, was slightly out of his mind. To see *sebastos* in a person was to observe the god in him, his sanctity. A man who possessed *sebastos* may well have been someone capable of mantic behavior, and so able to practice divination. Socrates might well have realized that in Parmenides' presence he was dealing with a man who knew important things, and who had experienced a profound revelation at some point in his life. It was one that not even he, Socrates, was familiar with, in spite of his own occasional trance-like behavior which others had later observed in him.[11]

For Parmenides to come to Athens to defend his own poem, even if it were different than the version written by Zeno, meant that he knew how important it was. So did Socrates and later Plato, who reported their meeting in his Dialogue. I do not wish to explore, at least not yet, what lay at the heart of his poem, which both Athenian philosophers thought so important. What I want to do is create the circumstances under which this meeting took place, for it is one of the great moments in the history of philosophy. One can talk about the time when Fichte and Schelling met, or perhaps Nietzsche and Wagner, but these do not seem so momentous. No actual

• • • • • • • • • • • •

11 The Greeks have another word that describes such a condition: *thambos*. It designates a kind of 'sacred terror' which one feels at the approach of a person charged with supernatural energy.

text such as the *Parmenides* was inspired by these encounters. No profound insights were to be aired that would change the course of history. Because these men were already enclosed in their own worlds, poetically as well as philosophically.

Parmenides approached Socrates that day with 'the depth of his mind' evident in his demeanor. He was a magnanimous man, an *adoleschia*, who left the younger man feeling overawed. No easy feat, I suggest, to achieve with a man like Socrates. Socrates had met his match. Here was the man. Here too was a man who had plunged into the darkness of illusion and false appearance, and come out on the other side. No man had articulated such a vision of otherworldliness before, not even Pythagoras.

Parmenides final remarks to Socrates at the conclusion of their discussion reflect where he had been, and from where he had emerged. 'If there is no one, there is nothing at all. Whether there is or is not a one, both that one and the others alike are and are not, and so appear and do not appear to be.' Here is the crux of the Parmenidian riddle: what is, is; what is not can never be. It is none other than an ancient Greek *koan*, and a lifetime is required to plumb its meaning.

This was the place I was committed go. I don't know why, but the fact that here was a poem that *I could not understand* left me in no doubt that there was work to do on my part. As there was work to do for Socrates and later Plato who made Parmenides' thought central to their own. Let's be frank about this: as much as we revere both philosophers for their contribution to the great adventure of western thought, we should always remember that these men stand on the shoulders of Parmenides. He is their mentor.

Poetry is the hero of philosophy. The world's destiny is linked to poetry. When we begin to think about philosophy, we begin to realize that it has a mystical element to it, which drives us towards the realization of a penetrating idea. It never ceases to drive us inwards in all directions as we struggle to find our footing. Philosophy is an act of self-liberation – that thrust towards understanding ourselves and the world. It has been suggested that philosophy is like a caress; it bears witness to the deepest love of reflection, to the absolute delight in encountering wisdom. A true philosopher cannot be discursive. He builds his universe out of mystical subtleties, what Novalis called 'logical atoms'. Only poetry can truly deliver such an outcome, this self-penetration of the spirit. A true philosopher, like Parmenides, *had* to be a poet.

To be a poet, then, demanded that I had to be a philosopher. Parmenides understood this fact to be correct when he first penned the *Way of Truth*. He knew that if he were to lift the veil concealing the invisibility of Being he must resort to a language sharper than any rapier. He chose metaphor, the word that cuts through reason, no less than the frisson of intellect when confronted with the elusive nature of the word. He chose poetry as his form because he realized that even his capacity to think through an issue would not sustain the sheer enormity of what he had to say. Did not Dante abandon writing philosophic tracts such as *De Monarchia* in order to write the *Divine Comedy?* And did not Boethius do the same when he wrote *Consolation of Philosophy?* He blended poetry with prose just as Dante did when he earlier wrote *La Vita Nuova* earlier in his career.

Parmenides compelled me to embrace incomprehension as a condition of understanding. What you do not know, what cannot be known, is like a candle guttering on the other side of a window. It glows, it beckons, even as its flame begins to waver. I could never know what Parmenides was trying to say unless I dedicated myself to dealing with the confusion of not knowing. How can this be? Aren't we conditioned to living our lives by way of the known, the factual, whatis visible and present? Of course we are. The entire premise of western society is based upon us dealing with what is securely evident. Yet this man, Parmenides, had the temerity to call our bluff. He told us that only what is Real is, while the world we know and deal with every day, is not. It is all an illusion.

We should not forget that he was an initiate of Apollo. We are told that to know Apollo demands the highest style, and to understand the god as an exaltation above everything human. Apollo is ennobled by loftiness of spirit. He is the god of healing, and for Parmenides as an *ouliades,* a spiritual healer, there is a synergy. Cleansing the imperfections of the soul and spirit are central to Apollo's role. As an *ouliades,* it was also central to Parmenides' role too.

This is probably why Socrates noted his 'awe-filled presence' when they first met. He could detect the dread that accompanied his persona. Apollo was also known as the 'founder of ordinances' - that is, he was the overseer of authority and legal institutions in a state. We know that Parmenides framed the laws of Elea for his father. Nor is it an accident that the philosopher chose to attend the Panathenaic Games in Athens, as this was very much a part of being a follower of Apollo, the guide of noble and manly athletes.

We are seeing another side of his personality. He is not just a philosopher, but a man in league with youth. He doesn't mind enjoying the suppleness of limbs as they go about the business of performing feats in the gymnasium or on the field of competition. Beauty doesn't always lie in a well executed statue, but also in ephemerality, the swift movement of a young man running or tossing the discus. Is this not what we enjoy most when we attend a sporting event? Parmenides knew well enough that the life of a man glides away like a shadow. If it is to shine, it is because of a light from above that gilds it. That light is the laurel crown bestowed upon young men by Apollo, Parmenides' tutelary protector. What dread he possesses is a gift of a god.

I emphasize these points of character because I feel they help me to draw nearer to just who was this man Parmenides. History offers but a few scraps from the table. Apollo is a bow bearer, capable of shooting from afar. Foresight *(phronesis)* is one of his greatest attributes. He sees from afar, just as a philosopher should. In spite of his Olympian presence, Apollo strikes us as a god able to proclaim the presence of the divine not in the miracles of a supernatural power, nor in the rigor of an absolute justice, nor in the providence of an infinite love, but in the victorious splendor of clarity where order and moderation hold sway. These are the qualities that Parmenides inherited from Apollo. To paraphrase Pindar, who knew well of such things, a trembling seizes us when we enter the abode of a god. In Parmenides presence, as Socrates discovered, the world begins to tremble.

III

Our philosopher partook of the ancient practice of *hesychia*, the discipline of stillness. It was a method of contemplation that allows a man to draw near to the divine world of the gods. It is a term not unfamiliar to me after a lifetime of visiting Orthodox monasteries in Greece and Egypt. The term was used by Evagrius Ponticus, an early Christian thinker, who often articulated such a discipline in his writings. In a state of *hesychia*, a man hopes to attain to a stillness that transcends all understanding.

Hesychia was a discipline that was said to have originated among Egyptian solitaries long before it was given a name in Greek. Anthony, a fourth century anchorite who lived in a cave in the Eastern Desert for more than fifty years, was a master of *hesychia*. The practice was said to have been a part of a meditation technique practiced before the arrival of Christianity. Which sets it back even further in time, probably to the time of Pythagoras, who travelled to Egypt to study with priests loyal to the old Pharoanic religion, where he would have encountered such practices.[12]

I have no proof that Parmenides was a *hesychast* other than the hints that I had read in his poem, and in his early life. If it is true, and I suspect it is, not least because his teacher Ameinias was a Pythagorean, it stands to reason that he taught Parmenides through oral transmission many of the secrets of the sect. Such men, known as *Acusmatici* (from *akousma*, meaning 'oral precept'), chose to emphasize the observation of a special Pythagorean way of life taught by the Master himself. The ancient discipline of *hesychia*, which originally drew its inspiration as a practice of recluses who spends long periods meditating in caves (such as Anthony), made it possible for them to experience a state of mind not open to people living in the idea of here and now.

The idea of the cave as a metaphor for descent goes back to Homer and the *Odyssey* where he makes light of it as the home of nymphs. Porphyry, a third century Neoplatonist, gives us a different perspective on the cave. He tells us that it is both a 'gate of men' and a 'gate of gods', that it has two entrances, not one. It is the place where men and gods are able to commune, acting like a vortex: what lies outside the cave entrance extends into

....
12 In Iamblichus' *Life of Pythagoras*, we read: 'He also build a cavern out of the city, adapted to his philosophy, in which he spent the greatest part of both the day and the night; employing himself in the investigation of things useful in disciplines, forming intellectual conceptions after the manner of Minos, son of Jupiter [Apollo].'

the broad mass of the world, and so exemplifies the realm of matter, of multiplicity and the manifold.

Inside the cave, inside its concavity, lies another realm – of darkness and the knowledge of ancient wisdom that may be of Zoroastrian origin, as Proclus tells us. Plato alludes to this fact in the *Republic* when he says, 'Behold men, as if living in a subterranean cavern, and in a den-like habitation, whose entrance is widely expanded to admit light through the whole of the cave.' That light is 'the light of the sun'. Again, this is another reference to Phoebus Apollo, the sun-god.

For all that, I do not see Parmenides as a cave dweller. He is too much the aristocrat and man of the city. He who frames laws and participates in public life as one of its councilors is not the sort of man who retires to a cave. But I do see him utilizing the principles of *hesychia* in the quiet of his own home. I see him as a retiring sort of person once his public duties have been fulfilled. Old Ameinias is ever at his side, even when he is no longer there. His study is filled with tablets and scrolls, as well as letters written to him by philosophers in Ionia and Athens with whom he corresponds.

They know of his work. They are familiar with his poem. Everyone is talking about it because it has broken with the tradition of *physis* that is the foundation of Ionian scientific thinking in the East, in what we know as eastern Turkey today. The iconoclast in him has made it possible for a new dispensation to emerge about how the world works. It is no longer just about the four elements, of fire, earth, air, and water, as the principal ingredients of physical reality. It is no longer about Love and as the binding forces that allow these elements to function as the basic building blocks of the universe, either.

Something new has entered philosophy with the creation of the *Way of Truth*.

That something was the notion of the metaphysical. Parmenides had decided that the workings of *physis* was not sufficient to explain the creation of the universe. Nor would he allow the old gods of the Olympian pantheon to interrogate reality as they had done in the past. Myth, as beautiful as it had been as a method of explaining the miraculous, simply did not have a place in his thinking. He did not despise or ridicule the gods; he simply declared that their place in the scheme of things was too palpable a reminder of the old Homeric virtues and the tradition of the epic as a repository for explanations that could no longer stand up to serious analysis. How the world was, this needed a more rigorous approach than the methodology of Ionian science or heroic Dactylic hexameter, the tool that Homer had made his own.

Metaphysics and logic, these were groundbreaking tools used by Parmenides instead. The word 'metaphysics' is important to our discussion as it has become much disparaged in our own time. In Greek, *ta physika* leads us to a study of the realm of nature, of inanimate bodies, plants, and animals, and is the basis of early science. We accept it as the essential nature of the physical world, and we feel secure within it. So did the Greeks. They had no argument with the physical as the basis of the real, and of beauty itself. But when it came to asking the basic question about what is the realm of being as such, its physical entity as they knew it did not embody a sufficient answer. Philosophic inquiry required more, even for the Ionians and their reliance on the four elements to bolster their ruminations on the nature of reality. They wanted to reach beyond *ta physika*, a place that few had gone to in the past other than through religious practice and the Orphic mysteries, at least not in Greece.

Meta ta physika was the answer they were seeking. That is, to go beyond the physical domain in pursuit of truth. 'Why are there essences rather than nothing?' is the fundamental question of metaphysics. To ask such a question is to go beyond *physis* and begin to deal with the essence of being itself. The Ionian philosophers of Parmenides' homeland in Phocaea and Ionia had not ventured into this region; rather, they were content to explore *physis* as being the essential ground of reality. Although, in fact, they did acknowledge *physis* possessing a soul-substance that made it more than just nature as we know it, their atoms were regarded as degenerate forms of divine attributes, a kind of 'spiritual' decay. Democritus tells us that souls was 'like motes in the air', capable of being breathed in in order to promote life.[13]

- - - - - - - - - - - -
13   Cf. We are also told that these motes are like 'sunbeams falling through a window', (Aristotle, *De Anima* 404a 2 - 4), which, in their own way, reminds us of the trajectory of neutrinos as depicted in modern particle science. Neutrinos are said to be massless, and able to pass through objects in a similar way as soul - substance does for cosmologists such as Democritus.

Nonetheless, they did ask themselves whether the four elements, as well as Love *(Philotes)* and Strife *(Neikos)* working in tandem: were these not enough? Was this not a perfect equation for being? Certainly for men such as Thales, Anaximander, Heraclitus and Anaxagoras, it was sufficient. They were cosmologists more than they were metaphysicians. Aristotle went so far as to call them *physiologoi* - that is, men who explored nature only. They were content to remain within the realm of science.

It is for this reason that Parmenides appears out of the darkness of thought like a comet. He chooses to ask a fundamental question, 'why are there essences rather than nothing?' He wants to bring beyond-ness into play, the *meta* of thinking as a valid exercise in coming to terms with the mystery of being. He wants us to think *metaphysically*. It is an important moment in the history of philosophy. A man has stepped forward to question being as mere *physis*, and to ask another important question: what lies *behind* being itself?

It must be remembered that metaphysics and philosophy are not sciences at all, at least not in the true sense, and in the sense that we know them today. So that Parmenides' break with the Ionian philosophers constitutes a break with early 'scientific' thinking. For him the nature of being could no longer be regarded as a sort of vapor, drifting about in his mind, or lying tethered solely to *physis* as the Ionians believed. He realized that if one was to understand the true nature of reality, one had to find another way of addressing the problem. He also realized that something important was missing from any attempt on his part to objectify reality as a constituent of nature only.

What was missing? If the gods had been deprived of divine attributes after the emergence of critical thinking, and the new science was already stripping bare the poetry of being as exemplified in the works of Homer, what was left? The answer was: spirit. The awakening of spirit as its own reality took its departure from the realization of scientific thinking and the gradual loss of the gods.

Something new had entered men's thinking for which the realization of a new metaphysic, an Absolute, becomes necessary.

People like Parmenides, in spite of his sophistication and logical mind, understood that spirit was not mere empty cleverness, nor the boundless work of dismemberment carried out by intelligence, nor was it a belief in world - reason. He knew that spirit was a fundamental, knowing resolve towards understanding the essence of being. Furthermore, that spirit was a mobilization of the powers of the essence of things as such, as well as a wholeness, what the Greeks call *oulomeles*, a completeness of Being itself. Where spirit prevails, the essence becomes at all times more essential to the right conduct of thought. To ask what 'being' is, even at its most basic level as it pertains to *physis*, becomes one of the fundamental conditions for an awakening of spirit. The spirit acts upon reality, and our thoughts, outside the forces of determinism and logic. Spirit is the mysterious 'other' central to the generation of a metaphysic, a beyondness of being.

The Greeks understood being as an uprightness, a standing - upright. But this standing - there, this coming upward, always remains in the domain of standing. It represents an intrinsic stability that encounters freely and spontaneously its own limit. It is not a limit that comes to essence from the outside, nor is it a deficiency in the sense of harmful restriction. The essence of being gains its authority from outside the limit. Limit is where the essence of being begins to *be*. Parmenides knew that in order to establish being as a metaphysical entity, he would have to resort to another mode of inquiry that precluded such concepts as the four elements or the forces of attraction and repulsion as indicated by Love and Strife.[14]

Parmenides needed to find a different method to help him structure his thought. He could not go down the road of delivering information and new knowledge by way of prosody, either. This would have forced him to mount arguments for or against, to enter into a dialectical process, as others before him had done. Nor could he simply write an epic poem in the tradition of Homer.

This meant he would have to create a new language to depict what he wished to say. In a certain broad sense he would have always looked upon language from a visual

• • • • • • • • • • • • •

[14] Neikos is the personification of hate and strife for Hesiod. He is the principle of repulsion and separation, the antithesis of Philotes (Love). Neikos causes the cosmos and the current world to be created from the sphere of One, where all the forces are mixed together. His action is one on repulsion in contrast to Love's expansive nature.

point of view, as most Greeks did, for the language itself was derived from the fluidity and openness of the sea, so central to the idea of being Greek. But he would also have to ask himself a question in the face of such a constraint: can I make the poetic image into a vehicle for expressing the essence of being and the reality of not - being as a reflection of the most important question of all: How does one determine, not 'being' so much as Being itself?

It was the question that defines the genius of Parmenides. It is easy to say that he merely wrote 'another poem'; it is not so easy to see this poem as an historic moment in the advent of primordial thinking. Before Parmenides, men could think cosmically through a reliance upon their epics, their stories, their histories of the gods, and how these played out in their everyday lives. After all, these were the bedrock of Greek culture.

Once the *Way of Truth* had come to fruition, this was no longer possible. Parmenides had closed the door on mythopoeic thinking with devastating consequences. I do not mean 'devastating' in terms of destruction or havoc *(alethros)*, but devastating in terms of the overturning of an entire cultural edifice that had been in place since the Greek alphabet had first become a vehicle for expression in the eighth - century BCE. The written word was now aligned to logical thinking as distinct from the old order of mythopoeisis and oral expression. The mold of early Greek life had been broken, and a new one was in the process of being fashioned.

In order to try and untangle my thoughts on the matter, I needed to return to Socrates' observation about Parmenides when they first met. There may be a clue lying underneath his remark that I probably hadn't thought about. If the man had 'filled him with awe' as he said, did he mean something more than the idea of dread being present in his countenance? Did he mean that Parmenides, by his dignified manner and awe - filled nature, was in fact displaying another quality, that of the uncanny? Had he been pierced by an arrow from Apollo's bow? I say this not as a metaphor, but as an actuality. Did he receive his knowledge from Apollo himself?

The uncanny is the simple, insignificant, ungraspable aspect of the will that withholds all artifices of calculation. It exceeds all planning. The uncanny is a transcendent event lying outside the realm of *physis*. The uncanny bestows upon the ordinary a condition that raises it into the extraordinary. The uncanny is that from which everything ordinary falls away. For a place to be regarded as 'uncanny', for example, it must emit a power in presence that is indefinable. Some ancient temples retain such a quality, as do a few living churches and sacred grottos. A spiritual residue exists in these places. For a man to be in possession of the uncanny, it must mean that he has undergone some form of initiation into an altered state. Shamans experience such a transformation, as do dancers when they become ecstatic. For a short while they are no longer themselves. The have entered into the domain of the uncanny.

Parmenides might well have experienced such a transformation. Not in any shamanic sense, but in the intellective sense. His transformation was supremely intellective, brought on by an encounter with some deep truth that had not been expressed by another man before him. He had been pierced by an arrow, the arrow of a god. He admits as much when he scolds Socrates for not entering into the spirit of philosophy in the way that he should. 'When you are older and more serious in your intent,' he seems to be saying, 'then you might be fortunate enough to encounter the uncanny.' When a god reveals itself *(to the ion)*, then will you understand what it means to know the divine. The god will have revealed itself in all its uncanniness. It will have appeared and transformed you into a *hemitheos*, a half - god.

I have met men who have demonstrated the uncanny, and they seemed to me to be half - gods. On my journeys among traditional peoples in different parts of the world I have come across men who filled me with dread - and who, at the same time, radiated an ethereal quality. I did not fear them so much as I was in awe. They radiated a presence, suggesting that they had been to another place. They had experienced a transformation in their being. Sometimes their eyes looked wild, at other times it was their gravity that made an impression upon me. They were not of this world. They had been touched by a god, and had become in their own way a *hemitheos*. Indeed, they *looked* uncanny. Why this should be so I was never able to determine. I merely accepted the advice that I received from others: 'This man is a spirit - man. He knows things because he has died and come back to life.'

These men endorsed the primacy of spirit even as they embroiled themselves in their ancient myth - life. I have no sense that Parmenides wanted to distance himself from Apollo just because he had chosen another order of thinking. He was pledged to the god through his Phocaean inheritance, his family culobjects, and his position as an *ouliades,* a healer, just as Apollo was. His respect for Delphi and the Pythian sibyl would have gone unchallenged throughout his life, given that Elea, his hometown, had been founded on her good advice. Like tribal peoples that I have met in the past, he was quite capable of living inside two dispensations: that of the gods as a repository of sanctity for all Greeks, and his commitment to the reign of intellect and the inner logic of metaphysics. Parmenides was no ordinary man: he had entered the cave, had experienced darkness there, and understood how the world of the uncanny can accommodate the contradictory. He could not turn back from his quest.

What I was beginning to realize is that gods are deprived of divine attributes according to the measure of a man. He determines whether they are able to come near or not. The gods are not 'there' for humankind, but for themselves. If we choose to make them a part of our lives, then they will draw near. It is this drawing - near that Parmenides refuses to dismiss since he never at any stage attempted to 'calculate' the reality of their existence. This was not his way. He could live in their presence as the *Way of Truth* attests.

He invokes the Goddess in the first lines of the poem. Like Boethius after him – he, an early Christian and also a classical Greek thinker at one and the same time, who summoned up the goddess Sophia to help him write his *Consolation of Philosophy* in his hour of need - Parmenides did exactly the same.[15] He did what Dante did also when he summoned up the divine Beatrice to accompany him on his journey through Heaven. The practice of drawing inspiration from a goddess was considered normal to those people who understood the nature of *iotores* – that is, the bringing-into - view of a god.

I can't help thinking that I am as if walking out on a pier into a bay that threatens to collapse under my weight. A man like Parmenides questions every certainty that I know. The power of his poem is that it abandons certainty except when it pertains to what he calls the 'One'. He does not mean number, either. His One is an absolute, unmitigated wholeness *(holotes)*, a supreme absence of multiplicity in the wake of its unmoving nature. To draw such a conclusion from a whole history of gods and their doings meant that he had to find another way to enunciate

· · · · · · · · · · · · ·

15 Boethius, (c. 480–524 ACE), was a Roman philosopher of the early sixth-century ACE. He entered public service under King Theodoric the Great, who later imprisoned and executed him on charges of conspiracy. While in gaol awaiting death, Boethius composed his *Consolation of Philosophy*, a philosophical treatise on fortune, death, and other themes, which became one of the most popular and influential works of the Middle Ages.

the concept of Being that lay beyond - or behind - being itself, under the predication of it remaining in a state of enduring absence, and forever. This took some doing. He it was, not me, who walked out on that pier one day, knowing that it would not collapse under the weight of what he had to say.

The question of being, and more pertinently, the question of Being itself, dominated Parmenides worldview. He could not get them out of his thoughts. He was a man driven by a desire to find some sort of logical answer in metaphysics that would affirm worldness *(soma pantos)* as a contingency, as a constantly changing state with no basis in stability.[16] He knew how dangerous these questions were to the entire cultural edifice to which he owed his allegiance. He knew too that to suggest what constituted the world was *un*stable, no more than a transitory thing, would lead to people questioning their very existence. Even to suggest that a primordial Being, a One, stood alone in the cosmos, untouched by time, by birth or decay, and by any relationship with men, was to call into

---

16   Cf. Proclus: 'In conjunction with the universal Nature and Necessity, he fashioned the World Body *(soma pantos)*, the partible bodies, and delineated the heavens'.

question the reality of the gods themselves.[17] Zeus and his pantheon could no longer *be* any more, except in some metaphoric or allegorical sense.

Where did this leave me? Entering into the poem over again was the only alternative that I had. I could no longer put it aside as I might other poems that had touched me. Something more was demanded of me. To what map could I turn to for guidance along the way? Then I told myself: let the poem lead me intoits own light.

- - - - - - - - - - - -
17   One is the universal cause, the highest entity *(akrotaton)*. Prior to it there is no other principle save One. Being, on the other hand, is composed of limit and infinite, a unitary manifold *(plethos heniaion)*. There is nothing prior to Substance *(tes ousias)* unless it be supra-existent *(huperousion;* ie. transcendent). Immediately above and beyond Being is One, which is superior to Being and is Unity *(hen)* itself. The One is purely power, a causative force, not a 'thing' *per se,* whereas Being is a metaphysical substance, real existence unqualified lying outside One, but necessarily a part of One.

IV

Don't be afraid from engaging in inquiry
Nor let familiarity blind your gaze
Through the voice of gossip by tongue or ear;
Listen to well - argued proofs uttered by me.
Only one Way can be fruitfully discussed.

Here was my answer. Don't be afraid. Don't be afraid to go where Parmenides wanted me to go. But first I had to join him on his chariot and allow Apollo's daughters to bear me away from Night's abode, the home of uncritical thinking and the mire of opinion, the realm of appearance itself. According to Plato, the charioteer and his two horses represent reason, desire, and spirit.[18] Night, Parmenides tells us, is a dark place, a place watched over by stern Justice who holds the keys to a world beyond, where thinking and being are no longer confined by the exigencies of the everyday. This world, lying beyond

---

....
18   Cf. Plato, *Phaedrus* 496 a,b: [The soul]... 'let it be likened to the union of powers in a team or winged steeds and their winged charioteer... It is a pair of steeds that the charioteer controls; moreover one of them is noble and good [spirit]... while the other has the opposite character [desire]. Hence the task of the charioteer is difficult and troublesome.'

'cloud - lined gates' as it does, harbors something altogether different, uncanny. How does one persuade Justice to let me through? What do I have to give up?

Scholars argue that Parmenides is merely employing a literary device to engage our interest. By invoking the aid of a goddess, as well as Apollo's maids to soften Justice's heart, he is resorting to a convention established by Homer in his epic, *The Odyssey*. 'Sing in me, Muse, and through me tell the story,' the poet opens his epic. Boethius advises us of the "Muses' torn cheeks," at the opening of his great meditation, and Sophia or Wisdom's disgust at their frippery. What are we to think? That Muses of Poetry and goddesses are but a convention for poets of this time, as the scholars wish us to accept?

Some are quick to suggest that Parmenides adopted a form associated with Orphic apocalyptic poems of the sixth - century BCE. Somehow I can't believe this to be so. It is easy for us to say that a philosopher of Parmenides stature 'doesn't believe' in the gods, or that he is too intelligent to engage in such a metaphysical sleight - of - hand as that of resorting to an Orphic convention used by ancient poets. We must also understand that the concept of gods for the Greeks was neither personal nor theistic. Gods, after all, participated in the act of ensoulment.

'Lift the great song again,' Homer tells us, pleading with the Muse of Poetry. And why not? Parmenides knew that he could never reach the heights that he hoped to attain without divine help. Any poet worth his salt knows that, even in our time. 'Sing *in* me,' is a call for inner strength to overcome doubts. The voice of the Muse is the voice of mythos. Heidegger tells us that the look of a god who stems from Being can emerge *in* man, and can look out from the form of man in a way that articulates a particular vision.[19] That vision is informed by the gods.

This knowledge gives me reason to believe that Parmenides fully understood his relationship with the gods. They were not simply 'there' as a convention, but occupied a place in his heart. He did not 'believe' in the gods for the sake of his poem; they simply are. It is their are - ness that escapes our modern sensibilities. And yet I have experienced such are - ness among Aborigines in the Australian desert. They talk about their Dreaming spirits as being in possession of an are - ness, rather than occupying any part of the apparatus of belief itself. It doesn't occur to them to question their are - ness, even as they acknowledge with a good deal of pragmatism how the world works. They are not insensitive when it comes to analyzing nature's modes; but equally it doesn't occur to them to question the possibility that there might be two ways of viewing reality – a mythic or noetic one and a practical one, as determined by the senses.

As Heidegger remarks, Being *(Phasos)* can emerge *in* man. Being is the invisible architecture of the gods. It sustains them, it makes them palpable to our intellective sensibilities. When Parmenides tells us that he, the author of the poem, is about to pass through the gates of Night

• • • • • • • • • • • • • •
19   Martin Heideggar, *Parmenides*.

and Light to meet the Goddess, we know that he means it. He is not uttering a convention. He is invoking the aid of the gods. He knows that as a poet and not as a writer of prose he needs their help. He doesn't want to think or write discursively. He leaves that to other, lesser mortals such as his disciple, Zeno. Or Plato.

Poetry demands a special kind of dispensation to reach the heights of expression. Parmenides knows this. His contemporary, the poet Pindar, writes in one of his Odes that 'There is a time when men need most favoring gales/... But if by endeavor a man win fairly, soft - spoken songs/are given, to be the beginning of men's speech to come, and a true seal of great achievements.'[20] 'Most favoring gales' in this context is a way of invoking the gods. Yet Parmenides doesn't tell us who the Goddess is, at least not in the opening stanzas. We are left with the sense that she *does not wish to reveal herself* as a knowing form for fear of reducing her presence to that of a cipher, an allegory. Parmenides keeps us in suspense. He wants us to acknowledge the sanctity of the Goddess first, before we place too much emphasis upon her familiarity as a person. The philosopher is making sure that *we* remain in the realm of the uncanny for the duration of his poem.

I can deal with this fact because I have decided to remain attuned to the numen just as Aborigines are when they speak of their Dreaming spirits. They taught me

• • • • • • • • • • • • •
20   Pindar, Olympia 11. *The Odes of Pindar*. Trans. Richard Lattimore.

how to maintain such a sensibility against the backdrop of the here-and-now. I can leave myself when I allow the gods to enter me. I can put aside my consciousness, my selfhood. Primordial Being can take up residence in me, if I allow it. This is what Parmenides is telling me: that the Goddess, as yet unnamed, is a part of the divinization of being into Being. When that happens, then like Parmenides I can allow the Goddess to draw near to me through the aegis of his poem. I can become spiritualized by his words, the words of a vision bestowed on him by a goddess who was both a friend to him as well as being a psychopomp.

How does one extend one's hand to a goddess as Parmenides did? Did he do so in a trance, a dazed condition, or when he was in the full possession of his faculties? This question needs to be asked if we are to put aside once and for all the suspicion that the philosopher is dealing in allegory. Or did he not name her because to name her was to invoke the underworld, the realm of Persephone. In Parmenides' time she was simply known as 'The Mistress' or 'Maiden', thus alleviating the necessity to name her. She was the goddess of appearance, of death and rebirth, as one who weaves the garment of mortality while generating the delight of the senses. She is the first link in that chain extending from the depths to the heights, binding together beginning and end.[21]

- - - - - - - - - - - -

21 The goddess could also have been Theia, the Mother of the Sun, whom Parmenides might have interpreted as 'beholding'. This would place her well within the solar setting as depicted in his poem.

For her to extend her hand to the young Parmenides after his journey through the gates of Night and Light (gates are also associated with her name, as are crossroads), she did so not in the context of death, but as an agent of rebirth, of transformation. He had gone down into the Hadean realm as someone who was beginning to 'die' to the world, just as an Aboriginal sorcerer was said to have 'died' before returning to his people as a healer.[22]

It is this side of Parmenides' journey that I needed to understand. A moment of revelation had urged him to extend his hand to the Goddess, and she to him. How many of us have ever had such a privilege? How many of us have ever thought it possible to be greeted by a goddess? Amid the flailing manes of horses, the sound of panpipes issuing forth from spinning wheels, all this excitement of a chariot rumbling towards a broad and unending expanse, is this not a moment to be savored? To be touched by a goddess! It is at this point that I realize the monumentality of the poem. Parmenides is not using the device of poetry as might Pindar or Homer. He is utterly unselfconscious as to his role within the poem. He is living inside it as a man wrestling with the power of words to invoke the Goddess herself.

· · · · · · · · · · · · · ·

22   Heidegger identifies the anonymous goddess with Aletheia (Truth), other commentators with Hecate. Hecate was the patron of pathways and crossroads, which fits nicely with her appearance before Parmenides. He is at a crossroad. The etymology of her name reflects her character; 'She who operates from afar,' or 'the far-darter'. Hecate is said to have her origin in Caria, the land where Parmenides' forebears came from. She is also associated with Persephone.

And then she speaks to him:

> Welcome, young man, you who have come to my abode
> On a chariot driven by immortal maidens!
> It is no ill luck but Truth and Justice who urged you
> To travel on this Way. It lies a great distance
> From the beaten track of ordinary men.

At once I am aware that Parmenides has been chosen. A goddess has approached, and named two other goddesses, Aletheia and Dike (Truth and Justice), as those who urge him to embark upon his great journey. He is no longer in control of himself, but at the beck and call of Olympian Immortals. And what is this Way that they speak of? Obviously not a pathway that normal people take during their lives. Parmenides is being asked to separate himself from the usual course of events that frame the conduct of life, and explore another path. The 'frame', if you like, might well be a Pythagorean injunction to live a simple life, to practice meditation *(hesychia)*, and to eat unadorned foods as they did. It might also be an injunction to become an itinerant philosopher or peripatetic, which Parmenides is said to have engaged in at various times during his life. His voyage to Athens to meet with Socrates is one such example of his wanderings.

The Way, however, means much more than a style of life. It represents a distillation of alternative strategies for perceiving reality. Not just the world in its worldness, but the world as a metaphysical condition that transcends every atom from which it is made. Parmenides' encounter with the Goddess is unlike any other encounter in the history of Greek tradition or lore. Men might meet with gods as they do in Homer's epics, as strangers or behind veils, but it is always with a view to enlisting their help and succor. In difficult circumstances men need to invoke the support of a god. Men are weak; gods are strong. Ergo, help is on its way. But in Parmenides' case help is of another order. It is not about advantage or being saved. It is about changing the entire edifice of thought to which the Greeks had grown accustomed, in order that a man might free himself from his dependence upon being-in-the-world as a lived reality.

A forbidding prospect. Not to be in the world. And yet, to *be* in the world at one and the same time. The Goddess is pleading with Parmenides, who is still a young man (as yet, awe and dread are not a part of his demeanor), and so to embark with her on a new way of being and thinking. Not becoming, not advantaging, but 'being'. For the young philosopher, a man loyal to Apollo as Parmenides was, the Goddess is asking him a fundamental question about existence: *pos bioteon,* how should we live? In contrast, for the Goddess, truth itself is ever in danger of being extinguished. Why? Because for the most part men are content to watch the sun setting on truth than they are capable of enduring what the philosopher Damascius in the first century BCE regarded as the brilliance of its 'divine dawn'.[23]

- - - - - - - - - - - - - -
23   Damascius *Phil. Hist.* 36 BC.

The way that Truth and Justice urges Parmenides to embark upon is a journey homeward – a journey from darkness into the intelligible light. In Greek, the word *nous* means 'mind', and is related to a similar word, *neomai*, which means 'to return home', indicating a return from the darkness of death into the true life. Only a life lived according to intellect has stability, and is precisely the kind of philosophic life the Goddess wants Parmenides to share, in keeping with his own noetic consciousness. That is, through the intervention of her divine grace. In this sense, and in this sense only, does the Goddess come to Parmenides' rescue and extend her hand to him. She is asking him to use all his faculties in a very pure sense so that she might finally unveil her gift. Such is the Way, a realization of gnosis. Only in an ascent following a descent into hell can a man learn how to live the genuine philosophic life.

I now begin to glimpse what Parmenides' poem is asking of me. Not to sally forth into analysis, or to distance myself from engaging with gods because of any skepticism on my part. I must, like Parmenides before me, press on along the Way, and begin to understand the depth of his remarkable revelation. It is a task that demands a great deal of me. Like him, I will have to quit the beaten track and find my own way. And, like him, I must ask Dike, Aletheia, and the mysterious 'Mistress' to guide me. This is not an intellectual exercise, or a poetic one. There is far too much at stake to succumb to old strategies that might deliver a measure of comprehension only.

I am being asked by the philosopher to go beyond all rational expectation in the hope of receiving the gift of the Goddess herself.

Surely such a journey is worthy of someone who calls himself a man, I tell myself. What is known as 'divine', Parmenides seems to be telling me, is itself ineffable, a supra-existential condition pertaining to unity. He is also asking me to participate in what is its distinctive properties because these alone have the capacity to renovate my thinking about the world. He is saying: give the gods their due. To do so it is to learn how to live with them, and so become ensouled. To climb aboard his chariot, therefore, and proceed towards the Light, is to set out on a journey away from the yawning chasm of non-existence. It is at this point that I begin to understand that outward things can no longer touch me.

V

> You must now learn many new things, &
> Crack open the shell of truth well concealed
> So that men's opinion might best be understood
> As no true belief at all.

Here lies the nub of Parmenides' argument. He had been asked to be wary of men's opinion and the accumulation of knowledge that accompanies it. Truth is a goddess, and remains for the most part veiled. Aletheia as she is called, is known in Greek as the capacity to unconceal or disclose if the situation warrants it. Though Truth remains concealed, it can be wrenched from this state by conflict. Truth doesn't give herself easily because her primordial essence is always conflictual. Strange as it may seem she needs to be ravished, brought into conflict. This is what happens when we perceive ourselves living in a state of falsehood. We wrestle with our conscience, our circumstance, the very essence of our existence.

To begin that journey we must learn new things. We must find ways to crack open the shell of truth, and allow it to come forth as a realization that common opinion cannot be the basis of truth. To do this, one must first travel to the *peirata* of the universe – that is, to the ultimate boundaries of existence.[24] Proclus tells us, after his reading of Plato's *Timaeus*, that our physical senses prevent us from making such a journey precisely because they force us to remain too attached to generation and plurality, what he calls 'multifarious life - modes'.

We must begin to realize that much of our life is an act of framing reality to suit our purpose, and not as Parmenides might hope - as an act of embracing the completeness of Being itself *(oulomeles)*. By un-framing our perceptions - that is, by engaging our noetic faculties in how we see the world - we open ourselves up to gazing upon what Proclus calls a 'luminous vehicle' (ie. none other than Plato's sphere) as a mode of detachment. Parmenides alludes to this sphere later in his *Way of Truth* as an example of Being grounded in all the beauty of equipoise:

> One is empowered by Limit, complete
> On all sides, like the contents of a sphere
> Rounded, equipoised, neither large nor small
> Reacting in all directions equally, inviolate
> Perfectly attuned to uniform without Limit.

Parmenides is asking much more of us. He knows that looking at the world with our senses is a process of discursive inquiry, no more. Another form of inquiry is needed, one of looking *through* the medium of our

---

24 The word 'universe' in Latin means 'unus' (one) and 'versus' meaning 'direction or place'. The universe has a limit; it is not unlimited space. (Plato, *Timaeas* 1.448-58)

senses, an entirely different mode. Plato likens this to gazing up at the sun and stars with our eyes, before transforming what we see into a recognition of Being (and what lies beyond Being), in the form of metaphysical knowledge. Such knowledge underpins our understanding of the sphere. It is not a 'round ball' as such, but a state of 'roundness' that empowers the idea of Limit existing in and through One. He wants us first to break with our normal state of mind and its dealings with the everyday world so as to proceed towards an acknowledgement of One as the essence of unity. 'There are names,' Proclus tells us, 'that are appropriate to each level of reality: divine names for gods, discursive names for the discursive intellect, and names rooted in appearances for sensible faculty.'[25] The 'divine names' he speaks of are grounded in metaphysics, in the language of the unutterable. We have to swim among words first, even at the risk of drowning.

We have to know also that words have their limits.

How we deal with the world as a state of non-being is at the core of Parmenides' thinking. Through *hesychia* he had broken with appearances, and reached out beyond the language of myth to express how he felt about One. In doing so, he resorted to the language of myth to help him in the early part of his poem. He had to find some sort of metaphysical connection through metaphor. Writing as a poet rather than as essayist demands a certain kind of language to play its

• • • • • • • • • • • • •
25 Proclus, *Plat. Theol.* 11.6.92.

part in revelation. The gods, just as the Dreaming spirits for Aborigines, must be present in language if they are to invoke their awful presence. Be assured, Parmenides is saying to us, language is god - filled, it is the ethos of spirit. He wants us to see words as configurations of fire and light. One is unutterable, and can only be known to us through the gods. It is, as Proclus tells us, prior to all oppositeness, a pure unity prior to all duality.

The language of metaphysics is no more than a prompting towards inquiry into something that exceeds description. The result of such an inquiry tells us more about our own state of ignorance than the goal of our search. The non-discursive intellect, or *noesis*, allows us to grasp at the intelligible forms within the domain of Being, as if 'by touch' *(kat' epaphen)*, and so become aware of One lying beyond all our capacities to perceive. Such an awareness of One is itself a hypernoetic reality derived from One's transcendent purpose. We need to recognize that when the Goddess takes Parmenides by the hand, she is reaching out from the domain of Being 'as if by touch'. At the same time she is bathing him in a metaphysical aura that will allow him to descend ever deeper into the task he has set himself. Truth has now become, for him, a divine uncertainty.

What Parmenides is searching for is a state of radiance and inner illumination, a vision, not an exaggerated or presential encounter with Being itself. He knows this to be impossible anyway, given that Being does not reveal itself in the world. To surrender to Being would mean to cease to exist altogether, and he is not about to do that. He is a man, not a god. He has a relationship with gods, but he also knows his place. Their principles, as divine as they are, are to help him modify his behavior in the world.

Unlike his predecessors, including the Ionian materialist philosophers such as Heraclitus, as well as Homer, Parmenides wanted to formulate a new way of dealing with reality that was metaphysical rather than beholden to the illusory nature of appearance. In that sense his thinking is revolutionary: for him, all the epithets attributed to the heroes of old were no longer enough to sustain a true existence. Because existence from hereon must be grounded in a metaphysic, in an understanding of the miracle and incomprehensibility of the unity of One, and no more in the common parlance of myth or epic, or indeed in any belief in the concept of one God.

The gods are both real to him and a symbolic screen *(parapetasma)*. They simultaneously reveal and conceal the nature of being and Being. This is because the image of One, constructed as it is in language, inevitably distorts and fragments whenever it is subject to analysis. The highest and most perfect life of the soul can only be on the level of the gods; this is why it becomes necessary to invoke them on occasions when one is attempting to go beyond ordinary reality. As does Parmenides at the outset of his poem. His soul is on notice as it finally abandons self-identity, setting him free to write a poem where subject and object, the high and the low, and all other contingencies that provide him with the capacity for discrimination, are fused into one overriding symmetry. These are the 'new things' that he must learn if he is to travel on the Way. Truth's shell might be a hard to crack, but armed with noetic perception and insight he is ready for the task.

The soul does not partake of individuality, for that too is an illusion. The soul, at least according to Plotinus, is a label for a variety of psychic and intellectual activities, not for a stable and permanent nature. The ordinary man is a 'pitiful fragment of the cosmos' in Plotinus' view, even though his soul is a part of One.[26] If he is to overcome multiplicity, of the 'two becoming one' *(ta duo hen ginetai)*, he must strive towards some sort of union with One. 'Where I begin is all One to me', so Parmenides tells us at the onset of his great poem. Such a condition of union *(henosis)* allows him to become a truly unified being, at one with himself and the cosmos, none other than what might be conceived of as a 'henotic' man. No philosopher before Parmenides had ever discussed such a condition. Prior to making his disclosure men were said to be on earth solely to engender the delights of appearance and the unlimited *(apeiron)*, to seek glory, and to honour the gods. Nothing more was expected of them.

Overcoming this 'scattering' of man in the manifold realm of appearance was central to Parmenides' view of

・・・・・・・・・・・・・

26 Prior to Plotinus, the soul was often regarded as a material not a metaphysical essence. Speusippus defined it as 'idea of the everywhere extended', and Xenocrates as 'self-moving number'.

humankind's destiny. He need look no further for confirmation than to Apollo and his unifying nature when it came to putting Dionysius back together after a period of non-reflection or 'scattering' in the world, due to his narcissistic isolation of ego. As Damascius relates:

> When Dionysius had projected his reflection into a mirror, he followed it and was scattered over the universe. Apollo gathers him and brings him back to heaven, for he is the purifying God and truly the savior of Dionysius.[27]

The soul is never united with the gods individually because it had no individuality. Like Dionysius, it has become fragmented. Only through awareness and recollection does it move from particularity to universality, from plurality to unity. Parmenides tells us very specifically about such 'scattering' as being a kind of Dionysian nightmare: 'Illusory/ is the nature of being when widely dispersed'. He is telling us that the road to hell is lined with those who have lived a fragmented life.

It is hard to imagine how Parmenides felt when others read his poem for the first time. They would have been aware of many of its sentiments due to their familiarity with Pythagorean doctrines derived from Egypt and elsewhere. The idea of *hesychia* as a discipline of meditation would have made them alert to the 'scattering' of soul - substance as a condition of the fragmented life too. Its message would have been imbedded in Orphic

---

27   Damascius, *In Phaed.* 1.129.1-4.

rites and practices long before Parmenides was born. But the directness of his statement 'illusory is the nature of being when widely dispersed' would have struck them as odd, to say the least. Theurgy and ritual, because of their reliance upon prescribed activity (song, procession to a sacred site, dance, the lighting of tripods in sanctuaries, incenses etc.), were the language of emotion rather than a precept for spiritualunderstanding with which they were more familiar.

One gets a similar impression of confusion from Plato when he recounts Socrates' meeting with the philosopher. Socrates and his friends wanted to dispute with him his theory of plurality, rather than to recognize that the 'plurality' Parmenides is talking about is the illusory nature of being when it becomes scattered. They continue to act as sophists who delight in argument for its own sake. It is then that Parmenides brings Socrates to task, as alreadymentioned: 'You are still young, and philosophy has not taken hold of you... Your youth makes you pay attention to what the world will think.'[28] Such is the talk of men who have yet to reflect upon the true nature of reality, of the unity ofOne itself.

Hodos, the sacred Way. This white-haired, dignified old man stands before me, even as he stood before Socrates in Athens. He is trying to get the younger man in me to understand what *hodos* means. 'Where I begin is all One to me' he keeps saying. I now begin to understand what he is trying to say. 'With the aid of your thoughts

- - - - - - - - - - - -
28   Plato, *Parmenides*. 130 e.

look seriously/at distant forms.' This is the moment when he begins to expound his metaphysic for the first time. He is on the brink of a new philosophic perception, one that will change the course of thinking in the western world. He is asking us to abandon theurgy, myth, folk belief, effigies of gods, temple precincts and all the paraphernalia of belief, for the sake of cutting - through by way of the intellect and the spirit in order to reach a more considered view of Being.

I am reminded of Christ's words during the Last Supper when he told his disciples that on this night at least, he would say it as it is. 'Until now I have been telling you everything in parables,' he said. 'Now comes the hour when I will talk to you in parables no longer, but tell you openly about the Father.'[29] Nomore stories, no more reliance on myth, let's talk about God (or One) as it is, Christ tells us. This is exactly the tone that Parmenides uses when he writes the opening lines of the *Way of Truth*.

> Never sever *what is* from remaining true
> To *what is*. Resist allowing it to be scattered
> Abroad as its opposite, *what isn't*. Illusory
> Is the nature of being when widely dispersed.

Here is the moment of revelation. Finally Parmenides presents his case for the reality of One as distinct from the usual reign of appearance. It is hard for us to realize how important this revelation is,

---
29 John, 16.25.

schooled as we are on centuries of Platonic theory and Christian exegesis on the nature of God's multiform, both in the world as Christ and as the Holy Spirit. The Christian Trinity has blurred the edges of our thinking in this respect. We accept the idea of a transcendent realm occupied by Deific presence. We accept too, on faith, that God entered history in the figure of Christ. For us to go back to Parmenides' earlier statement about *what is* means that we must tease out the question: What exactly does he mean by *what is?*

It is a question that has been on my mind for many years. When I first read it, I kept thinking in a materialist manner. *What is* is a clear statement about the palpable, the observable, and, so to speak, the touchable. The world and all that is in it, is. I had no conception then that what I perceive as the world contains nothing permanent, so that *what is* as I understood it to be assumes another condition, that of *what was* or *might be*. I firmly believed that all I see and acknowledge as having an objective reality as distinct from myself (as well as including myself) is a sufficient cause to be. The concrete nature of all that is in the world is firmly rooted in such an assumption: that it has always been there, that nothing changes except on the surface, which is little more than a process of interactive change.

Yet Parmenides wants me to believe that this assumption of mine is wrong. He tells me never to sever *what is* from remaining true to *what is*. Over the years I have struggled with such an apparent riddle. Because for me it was a riddle! Never break with the aeternality of isness in pursuit of its opposite, *what isn't,* the purely temporal, he seems to be saying. Again, what does he mean? I always thought of such a statement as merely being an expression of the negative, of the not - ness of things. A house is, or it is a hut. A wet day is, as distinct from a dry one, which it is not. That seemed clear enough, as well as being a reasonable basis for managing reality. I know what is, and I also know what isn't. At least I thought I did. The trouble was, I began to realize that Parmenides had another agenda in mind when he made this statement in the first place.

Parmenides wanted me to reconsider my attitude towards reality as an objective condition. He was asking me to put aside my ego, whose essence is largely subjective, in a bid to arrest the sway of consciousness that insists upon its capacity to deliver the perfect mode of being. To parody Descartes, 'I know, therefore I am'. It is in knowledge that I feel firmly grounded. To know a thing is to perceive its objective reality. But Parmenides is questioning this belief ofmine. He is telling me that it is none other than an expression of what Heidegger called the 'rebellious sovereignty of man'. We think we know. The essence of subjectivity is bound to the selfhood of man. Only in selfhood do we begin to perceive the world as a manifestation of knowledge.

Parmenides' contemporaries would have largely agreed with these remarks. They were materialist philosophers, after all. The four elements, as well as the activities of attraction and repulsion, these helped to make the world as we know it. It had no metaphysical basis to it whatsoever. It could be expressed in myth or story, but these were merely a device largely divorced from their sacral origins in ritual. What counted was the ground of things, the ordinary dimension to reality, which the Greeks term *episteme*. The *episteme*, according to Michel Foucault, is the 'apparatus' which makes possible the separation, not of the true from the false, but of what may be from what may not be characterized as scientific.[30] To break with this concept was to enter the metaphysical domain. And Parmenides had chosen to do so rather than to remain in the world of appearance and its illusory qualities.

He affirms his position when he reiterates: 'Where I begin is all One to me, & I will/return again & again to this refrain'. He is saying everything that is grounded in the Real, in One, is all of a piece, and is determined by a condition that transcends the illusory nature of being. His reality begins in the unity of One, the primordial Other, not in any scientific worldview which engages in the act of knowledge-seeking as a manipulatory act. He knows such a worldview exists, particularly among his contemporaries in Ionia, but he refuses to be seduced by their easy evaluation of matter as being a state of *what is*.

What is becomes a metaphysical reality for him, a condition that transcends process of any kind. According to Parmenides, humankind's being-in-the-world places him in the domain of history. But Being itself lies outside

- - - - - - - - - - - -
30   Michel Foucault, *Power/Knowledge*.

such a purview. One is not a contingency in time. It *is*, in its own sphere, not *of* anything. It is made up of *oulon*, what is homogenous and continuous. It has no past, no present, or any future. If someone wishes to reconsider his position as a part of history, and so dependent upon time, then he needs to re-appraise his relationship with subjectivity and with the ego. He must *stand outside himself* if that were possible, in order to attend to One as a primordial expression of *what is*. Only then can a man find himself enveloped in the Being-ness of his presence in the world. He has become an atom of Being, of One itself.

So here I stand. I have finally embraced Parmenides as a friend rather than a distant interlocutor across the millennia who happens to know quite a deal about Being and One. He now expects me to break with *physis* as the sole determination of being, and of being-in-the-world. His way of truth demands that I 'look seriously at distant forms' and see them as being 'close at hand'. This is a moment of truth for me. I have arrived at a point where I can no longer accept the 'beaten track' that he speaks of as the place where I should be. To do so, at least according to the philosopher, would be to condemn myself to the interminable round of seeming-to-be. What the Indian sages call Maya, or illusion.

VI

I now find myself entering deeper into the *Way of Truth*. Like Parmenides before me, I have accepted the hand of the Goddess. She is by my side as I negotiate the shoals of apprehending and being. When he tells me that apprehending *(noien)* and being are one and the same, I know that he wants me to believe that the isness of being is linked to the idea of it being thought, and never the reverse. Truth does not lie in not-being. That can never be considered as real. 'Is-not-ness' as a condition of being is unthinkable because it distances us from the reality of One. To cut ourselves off from Being is to allow ourselves to fall into the dark abyss of matter as something which is real. Parmenides does not want us to do that. Joy, the vivacity of life itself, these are inspired by a knowledge of One, of Being, he tells us. When Being is not acknowledged, then we are left to embrace the lumpish nature of ordinary being as no more than a transient thing.

Truth is embodied in isness, not in the relativity of questioning the nature of reality. To say that *it is,* is not to say that 'it exists', which necessarily partakes of another order of participation in the world. According to Parmenides, Truth is always and ever to be known as a transcendent reality, an aspect of One. Knowledge of it is determined by a supernatural light as distinct from the darkness of night, as his poem suggests. What is known at this level is always true. He is proposing a deific absolute as a condition of thought and being in the minds of mere mortals such as ourselves.

We must think Truth as a primordial existent *outside* our normal cognitive processes, which are linked to our ego and the demands of having and of possession. In contrast, as Plato suggests, that one who knows, knows something, which is acceptable at a factual level.[31] But when Parmenides talks about knowing, he really means that Truth embodies a knowing that is separate from our cogitations altogether. His Truth can only be known by a mind inleague with One – that is, a mind detached from the ego. A mind that is absolutely embodied by One's power to disclose through Being, like the Goddess herself when she offered her hand to Parmenides. This power is a demonstration of *oulomeles* no less, of Being in its completeness. All things that exist, do so by virtue of One,

---

31 Plato, *Republic* 477a.

so Iamblicus tell us.[32]

'*It is* can never be confused with not-being,' he tells us. What he fails to inform us explicitly about is that *it is* can never be confused with being, but he means it nonetheless. Being as being is a contingency, it thrives upon relativity and change. What *is not* can never 'be' at any stage because it is an erroneous condition if we continue to believe that it might be, leading as it often does to false opinion. Parmenides regards any obsession with not-being, with transience, and the lure of false opinion and mere knowledge for its own sake, as a pathway to perdition. Why? Because it leads us away from the contemplation of One, the primordial essence, and away from our understanding of *henosis*, of unity.

At no stage does Parmenides wish to urge us down the pathway of sophistry or mere knowledge - gathering for its own sake as a way to justify our place in the world. He wants us to be ever alert to the pitfalls that lie in wait if we pursue such a course of action. He pleads with us not to journey down that road. All the ills of the world are bound up in our being seduced by being and not-being as the basis of how we live. Either/or, Shall we?/shall we not? Are these not the rules that apply to the

----

[32] See Fragment 1, (Strobaeus, *Anthology 1.5.17*) 'Letter to Macedonius,' by Iamblicus: 'All things that exist, exist by virtue of One, and indeed the primal level of Being itself is produces in the beginning from One, and in a very special way the general causal principle receive their power from One, and are held together by it in one single embrace, and are borne back together to the first principle of multiplicity, as pre-existing in it.'

decisions we take whenever we embark upon any normal activity? After all, we are brought up to think this way – our parents, our teachers, our employers, they all tell us how to 'work within the system', as it is often termed.

Today, all life is governed by certainty, or the need thereof, rather than the beautiful uncertainty of *henosis*, of unity, which is imbedded in the mysterious activity of the opposites *(anti - theton)* working in tandem. To direct one's thoughts towards One, whether it be by way of spiritual practice or mystical understanding, is not considered a practical outcome for a successful living-in-the world.

We know that for Parmenides living-in-the-world is all about knowledge-gathering. It is not about associating with Truth. It is as if we have remained infected by Pilate's remark to the mob outside his palace when he sentenced Christ to crucifixion. 'What is truth?' he asked, thereby condemning the idea of an Absolute as something real to the domain of 'mere' metaphysics. For most of us, according to the philosopher, the 'bland celebration of/ The simple properties of existence' are enough. It is these that fuel our material aspirations, our economies, our pursuit of jobs and security for their own sake, as well as being a platitude to justify our daily need to survive.

Parmenides demands much more of us. Central to his demand is to un-confuse our minds of the plethora of impressions that serve to divert our attention away from contemplating One. He does not mean this in any religious sense, but he does mean it in the metaphysical sense. What he also means is that in contemplating One, the primordiality of Truth, we are engaging with the goddess, Aletheia. For Aletheia is the essence of Truth. A decision has to be made as to whether we concern ourselves with Being rather than not-being as the determining factor in our lives. When the Goddess appears before us she offers the indwelling light of herself as a guide. It is an act of self-shining on her part. This is why Parmenides places so much emphasis on her touch. Here touch is an act of self-shining.

To think about the unity of One does not demand a solemn approach or the pretention of erudition. Nor does it require a display of exceptional states, such as mystical rapture or reverie. Parmenides never asks anyone to become an ecstatic, but to think openly and to be mindful in the presence of Being. His view is an unusual counter to those who believed that the Orphic mysteries, for example, or that of ritual and elaborate temple worship, offer the only pathway to understanding One. The Goddess's concealedness is a part of her mystery, but it does not mean that it will be withheld if one reaches out. Her manner is a coming-forth, a growing into the mind of someone who is ready to received her gift.

This is precisely why Parmenides' approach is so different to other philosophers. He has exempted himself from the demands of ritual or the need to serve the gods in some formal capacity. It does not mean that he dismisses their presence in his life. He is fully aware of the importance of Apollo, given thathe is one of the god's most faithful followers, and of other gods also. He is appreciative of the need for ritual in the lives of ordinary folk because the emotion that it invokes is a substitute for the demands of *hesychia* as a discipline, which they might find too demanding. Besides, the gods have always been a part of his culture.

Parmenides is the first person in the history of western philosophy to explore what the verb 'to be' *(estin)* really means. It might sound like an unnecessary discussion to have in the light of his understanding of Truth. But if we are to fully understand from where the man was coming, we must listen to what he is telling us. Nor do I mean in the manner of the specialist who sees the verb as a major stumbling block to understanding just what Parmenides is saying. His understanding of 'is' is, when married to Truth, revealing of the nature of a thing, its genuine character. If a thing is, then it is never in a state of becoming. It must always remain what it is. Anything that is in a state of coming-to-be must necessarily not be what 'is'. While, for his Ionian friends, *physis* gives character to the thing, and substantiates it in the world as an object, for Parmenides this view was insufficient. For him, isness transcend all change, which was implicit in the Ionian philosophers' understanding of nature. In contrast, he believed that it must partake of an unchanging condition, never a coming-to-be.[33]

This fact is more than confirmed by the philosopher Simplicius when he insisted that Parmenides really

---

33   Patricia Curd, *The Legacy of Parmenides.*

did distinguish between the aeternality of a thing and its provisionality in the world. In his book *De Caelo*, he wrote:

> Those men posited two levels: that of what truly is, the intelligible: and that of what comes-to-be, the sensible, which they thought one should not speak of as 'being' *simpliciter*,[34] but as 'apparent being'. Hence they say that truth concerns what is, whereas opinion concerns what comes-to-be.[35]

Here we are close to what Parmenides was struggling to articulate: that a 'thing' when it resides in Being is different to a thing as a part of *physis*, of being as a coming-to-be. And what lies in Being is the truth of things because they are never coming-to-be in that they are, but are rather always of an isness. The Goddess says as much when she argues that *what is* is immovable, complete, and without end:

> ... being is indestructible
> Ungenerated, of a wholeness, immovable
> & without end. Nor *was* it ever, nor *will*
> It be, since it is always and forever *is*.

She wants us to consider that if thinking and being are one and the same, then there must be an even stronger claim to do with the fact that there does, and must be, something to be spoken and thought of first. She refuses

- - - - - - - - - - - - -
34   *Simpliciter* means 'artless' or 'natural'.
35   David Gallop, trans. *Parmenides of Elea*.

to allow anything not to exist other than *what is*. The path of *what isn't* is simply un-nameable. We cannot even think about it. What would be the purpose? he seems to be saying. If you do – and we do talk about *what isn't* in our daily lives all the time, absorbed as we are by the here - and - now – then all that is happening is that One is losing its primordial potency as the determining power behind the miracle of existence. And that is impossible.

There are writers who maintain that Parmenides attempted to allegorize our behavior, that his poem is a commentary on our irrational impulses and appetites. Sextus Empiricus, in his *Against the Mathematicians*, reminds us in his own way of how Dante viewed his role as a poet and allegorist when he penned the *Divine Comedy*. Sextus was quoting a fellow philosopher, Xenophon, who knew Socrates, and so was familiar with their discussions about the *Way of Truth*. Furthermore, he had written about Parmenides in his book, *On Nature:*

> For in these verses Parmenides means that the mares which carry him along are the irrational impulses and appetites of the soul, and that 'the much- speaking route of the goddess' they travel is that of inquiry according to philosophic reasoning; this reason, like a divine guide, points the way to knowledge of all things. And the maidens that lead him on are the senses; of these to auditory faculties in a riddling manner by saying 'it was urged on by two round wheels', that is with the circles of the ears, by means of which they receive sound; and visual faculties he calls 'maidens, Daughters of the Sun

leaving the House of Night' and 'hastening into the light', because it is impossible to make use of them without light. And the approach to 'much avenging Justice' who also holds 'the keys of requital' is the intelligence who holds a reliable apprehension of things. And she, after welcoming him, promises to teach him two things, 'Both the steadfast heart of persuasive truth', which is the immovable foundation of knowledge, and secondly, 'the belief of mortals in which there is no credence'. That is to say, everything which lies in the realm of belief, because all such things are uncertain.[36]

Sextus is writing long after Parmenides lived, more than six-hundred years, in fact. While his interpretation of the philosopher's poem is of interest to us, as it is derived from the work of a contemporary of Socrates, we must treat it with caution. At the time when Sextus wrote in Alexandria (c. 200 BCE), Christianity was an emerging religion in its own right, and was busily developing its own language. Its tenets were often interpreted in such a way, too – that is, allegorically. The old order of the Greek gods no longer held sway as they once did, so that when Sextus talks of the Goddess she has largely become a cipher for allegorical interpretation. For him, as for Xenophon, she has now become a literary device, and is no longer of the supernal order of One.

I do not believe this was Parmenides intention when he wrote his poem. It is easy in retrospect to read into

· · · · · · · · · · · · ·
36   *On Nature* 1. 1-30. Quoted by David Gallop, *Parmenides of Elea*.

his words another layer of meaning, to talk of Homeric precedence and the need to ground the poem in an older poetic tradition, including allegory. His description of the journey by chariot in the company of the Daughters of the Sun, and their subsequent encounter with the Goddess, are too vivid and immediate to be just another poetic device. It speaks of a poet who needed to invoke the aid of the gods, as he does throughout his poem, in order to sustain the full import of his revelation. He needs her help as he rumbles forth on his chariot into the region of One.

Ultimately Parmenides is telling all of us that we must make a decision about which path we should follow. At the same time, he is alerting us to the difficulties of that choice. Are we to abandon the 'simple properties of existence', those everyday pleasures that make life worthwhile? Is he telling us that this is the false way, the way of *what isn't?* Is his tone condemnatory of normal existence? Or is he just another fire-breathing prophet issuing a warning to us? My sense is that none of these questions are pertinent to how he wishes us to address the moral imperatives of which he intimates. He is simply stating a case for why we should address the greatest issue of all: is it possible to embrace and understand the role of One in our lives?

Plato struggled with this issue through his alter ego and teacher, Socrates, in his dialogue, the *Republic*. There, he tells us, that knowledge is matched by *what is*, and ignorance necessarily by *what isn't*. He then goes on to say that we need to search for something lying between knowledge and ignorance that itself contains them both, and so draws them together, a kind of *tertium quid*.[37] The scholars tell us that such a choice is one we make whenever we know something to be true, and follow it, or when we choose the path of ignorance and don't. Knowledge and ignorance are placed in opposition - which, they inform us, bothParmenides and Socrates sought to justify in their respective arguments by way of a paradox. The trouble with this argument is that it is rather too *intellectual*, the product of clear minds debating a point in logic.

Understanding the nature of Truth is not always about entering the field of logic, however. For all his brilliance as a logician, Parmenides is saying much more to us than the either/or, or a *what is* and *what isn't* that he sets up as paradigms. I would not have been so affected by his poem when I first read it all those years ago if it were merely to hear the voice of an ancient philosopher telling me a little about truth and ignorance. Something else was calling to me from the heart of his poem. I heard the voice of a man who had passed through those gates of Night and Light that he described because his life depended on it. He had gone through them because he needed to find a meaning to his existence. Nonetheless, by some strange twist of fate, he sensed that the gods had begun to fail him, to retreat from his life – why, he didn't quite know. Not in their emotional or cultural context, which he continued to acknowledge, so much as inthere capacity to define One, the Absolute, which he now discerned as being the most

. . . .
37   *Republic,* 476e-477b1.

important issue *to* understand.

No poet or writer before him had taken on such a challenge. It was a challenge, I suspect, that I now had to face 2,600 years later if I was ever going to understand the meaning of his poem. I needed to find out for myself why it had become such a profound hymn to the miracle of the universe, and why. The *Way of Truth* stands like a dolmen in a field, an ancient stone planted there as a revelation. Deciphering its relevance required another order of thinking, a thinking that broke with analogy or comparison. I had to ask myself whether I was capable of such a thinking.

VII

What is it that Parmenides found so compelling about One? To answer this question I needed to better understand his relationship with Apollo. As a 'son of Apollo' – that is, as an *ouliades* – he brought to his vocation as a philosopher a particular depth that was intrinsic to Apollo himself. Parmenides was more than just a logician, and his poetic language was derived from some intense inner experience. Apollo was the god of music and poetry, and so aligned to beauty itself. Pindar tells us that Apollo is honoured by the epithet *hagne*, which indicates his holy and pure nature. There is something mysterious and unapproachable about his nature that commands an awed distance. The same could be said about One; what empowers it is a certain stringency, a limit.

As an *ouliades*, Parmenides would have known the value of limitation. A man must learn to contain himself if he is to realize himself as a man. To overreach one's selfhood is to bury oneself in the unlimited. He tells us that the unlimited is a condition of anarchy, not autarchy.

How we deal with limitation is a mark of our ability to become self-contained. For Parmenides, this was also a quality of One: 'One is empowered by Limit, complete/ On all sides, equipoised, neither large nor small/Reacting in all directions equally, inviolate/Perfectly attuned to uniform without Limit.' He informs us that One *can* be extrapolated into being, into our everyday lives, just so long as we acknowledge the intercession of a god, in this case Apollo.

Phoebus Apollo, the pure. At once we are alerted to his celebrated maxim, 'Measure is best' *(metron ariston)* which greeted weary pilgrims at the entrance to his temple in Delphi where they went to consult the Pythian oracle. All is in balance, in equipoise, removed from any form of relativity such as large or small, high or low. These are the qualities of One, and also of the whole man. In this sense One is no longer remote from us. The God has revealed himself. 'Let me proclaim the unerring council of Zeus,' he tells us, informing humankind of the infinite power of One.[38]

Apollo's tools of trade are the bow and the lyre, one to deal out 'far shooting' death, the other to inspire us with his music. Of interest is the fact that Apollo does not sing as Orpheus does; rather, he brings forth melody only. Both instruments, the bow and the lyre, rely on the tension of opposites to achieve their effect. *Tormentum*, the Romans called it – that is, a way of achieving tension running between the bow and stern of a galley with a

---

38   Pindar, *Hymn to Apollo*. 3.

twisted rope tautened during rough weather. Things are held together through tension. The bow string and the lyre string, each delivers its melody because of tension. Apollo is the god of tension, though it is never said of him directly. His tension, however, is a positive one, the tension of limit. Like One, which is defined by Limit, so too is the God's decree.

We are nearer to understanding why Limit and One are so important, and so linked. Deific nature represents pure Limit, which holds things together in contrast to the Unlimited, which caused things to expand and change, to fall away. It is interesting to note that the ancient Greek word for the concept of surface limitation, that which holds things together in the world, was *chroia* or 'skin'. The idea of limit in the world was a kind of skin that preserves things for as long as they continued to exist as objects. When they decay in time, as they inevitably do, so do they lose the binding effect of their skin. They lose their form. The contrary nature of Limit and the Unlimited, the tension between them, produces the world as we know it. But it is Limit that presides over the Unlimited and allows it to operate within prescribed constraints, never the opposite. Limit and Unity are the overarching constituent of One.

He would have also been aware of the fact that One - the universe as its sole manifestation - actually *breathes*, at least according to his teacher Ameinias and other Pythagoreans that he might have known. I find the concept fascinating: that the universe breathes. It inhales the void, which is unlimited and so infinite, and transforms it into a limit within One's absolute essence. As One continues to inhale, so does space between all that exists in the universe begin to contract. An insuperable breathing-in and exhaling makes it possible for the whole of nature to be.[39] One becomes embodied in number, plurality, and difference quickly realized, and so a rose blossoms before our eyes. Through Limit and the inhaling of the void, One creates time and motion too.

It is a beautiful concept. Could it be in cosmological terms a distant echo of recent discoveries pertaining to dark matter? We are told by astronomers and astrophysicists that dark matter occupies ninety-five percent of the universe, which implies that such is its extent that One is still breathing in its emptiness to fashion what we know as the cosmos. One has an infinite capacity to transform the void into all the plurality of being. It goes on and on, across space and time, this miraculous inhalation on the part of Limit *(peras)*, in creating all that is *(apeiron)*, at least in Parmenidean terms. Nothing *is not*, as he says, it is all enfolded in One. We are living in a finite universe because of One's capacity to breathe it in, and so make of the void a limit.

Parmenides knew that it is not possible to worship One. One he likened to a sphere because he knew that

- - - - - - - - - - - -

[39] The concept of the universe breathing is a very ancient one, and can be found in Hindu thought. The sun is responsible for the breath of life, as we read in the Prasna Upanishad: 'So arises this universal life-breath which has every possible form, [including] fire'. It is the universal life-soul emanating (breathing out from) the sun.

he had to give it some form with which our faculties might engage.⁴⁰ He was fully aware of how our minds work, and how we need something palpable to dress up our most cherished beliefs. He also knew that One could not be construed as a god, or as a substitute for a god. The logic he imparted to his revelation forbade him from taking such a stance. Nor should we blame him for that. We should not argue: Well, your One is just an 'excuse' for a god or the articulation of an Absolute. That would be to take the wrong path, the path of *what isn't*. Because One stands outside all linguistic affiliations. It cannot be uttered; it *is*.⁴¹

The conundrum is that Parmenides boxed himself in through the use of his uncompromising logic. 'All things are no more than names/We attribute as truthful,' he tells us. It was his way of acknowledging the dilemma that his revelation had invoked. One is but a name, even if

• • • • • • • • • • • •

40   This description was later taken up by Plotinus in the *Enneads:* 'If you take a small luminous mass as centre and surround it with a larger, transparent sphere, so that the light within shows over the whole of that which surrounds it... shall we not say that the inner [luminous] mass is not affected in any way, but remains in itself and reaches over the whole of the outer mass. And that light which is seen is the little central body that encompasses the outer?' The distinguishing characteristic of such an 'emanation' is radiation from the centre. Such an emanation is the action of Love, according to Parmenides. (See Ch. 8). Also Diagram plates.

41   Parmenides was not the only philosopher of his time to suggest that the All could be described as a sphere. Xenophanes, a friend and possibly even a teacher of Parmenides, and a fellow Elian, proposed that God is one and incorporeal. It is said 'to have a body of spherical shape... and indeed, this body is identified with the physical universe.'

it does suggest a sublime notion. One as sphere is but an analogy, even if it does give our minds something to hold on to. One empowered by Limit, nonetheless, is a perfect expression of lyre and bow, both of which partake of what the Greeks knew as *apeiron,* the world of the boundless and the unlimited – our world. *Apeiron* gives us our use of opposites to determine the unlimited world of being.

The next question is: How did Parmenides' hope to escape his austere monism? My sense is that he chose to articulate the idea of beauty as his response. He does not use the word 'beauty' explicitly; but he does invoke its presence in the *Way of Appearance,* the second part of his poem, when he alludes to the 'flame of the sun' and 'Olympus' grave slopes', the 'moon's nightly peregrinations and round face' in describing the sky 'with all its signs'. This is the language of a poet, and it is the language of *apeiron,* which he knows is important to us. Even though he knows that all such expressions are contingent, and in no way do they exist, he is happy to pronounce them if it helps him to make his point. True beauty is an ideal form which resides in Truth. At this point we might like to hear what Plato wrote on the subject in his *Symposium* in order to get a better idea of what Parmenides meant:

> Whoever has been initiated so far in the mysteries of Love, and has viewed all these aspects of the beautiful in due succession, is at last drawn near to the final revelation. And now, Socrates, there bursts upon him this wondrous vision which is the very soul of the beauty he has toiled so long to discover. It is an everlasting loveli-

ness which neither comes nor goes, which neither flowers nor fades, for such beauty is the same on every hand, the same then as now, here as there, this way or that way, the same to every worshipper as it is to every other.

... Starting from individual beauties, the quest for universal beauty must find him ever mounting the heavenly ladder, stepping from rung to rung – and that is from one to two, and from two to *every* lovely body, from bodily to the beauty of institutions, from institutions to learning, and from learning in general to the special lore that pertains to nothing but the beautiful itself – until at last he comes to know what beauty is.

... if it were given to a man to gaze on beauty's very self – unsullied, unalloyed, and freed from the mortal taint that haunts the frailer loveliness of flesh and blood – if, I say, if it were given to man to see the heavenly beauty face to face, would you call *his*... an unenviable life, whose eyes had been open to the vision, and who had gazed upon it in true contemplation until it had become his own?[42]

Parmenides, I believe, would have concurred with Plato's analysis of beauty. His 'wondrous vision' of beauty has never been equaled. It is a beauty that draws its strength from Parmenides' One, and may well constitute the binding element lying between knowledge and ignorance which Plato speaks of in the *Republic*, a *tertium*

---
42   210e – 211e.

quid.⁴³ No one can gaze upon One; but we can be seduced by its reflection in the world. Parmenides was aware of this, just as the younger Socrates and Plato knew it too. They both found themselves drawn into the sublime notion of beauty as an existent in itself. And because it partakes of One, Parmenides knew that it reaches into our soul to vivify every aspect of our being.

The soul of beauty is more than an existent or aspiration for us. It constitutes the very foundation of our lives. We cannot live without beauty because, for all that fails us in the world - the non-isness of things, everywhere – we still harbour a desire to perceive ideal beauty. One is intimately bound up with ideal beauty, the Beautiful. Parmenides suggests as much in his poem. Though he is reluctant to wax lyrical we always feel the power of his constraint. The 'miracle of the moon' is not just an empty phrase for him; it is the beginning of a cosmological statement that puts a break on the enthusiasm of his Ionian counterparts, for all their interest in *physis* and the security of elemental solutions.

One imparts beauty, even though it is immovable, inviolate, and replete with fullness. Once again a paradox presents itself. If One is becalmed in isness, and does

---

43   *Republic*, 476e-477b1.
Note: A *tertium quid* is a 'third element' that helps two known elements to combine such as electron, which is an alloy of gold and silver. Cf. Tertullian, *Adv. Praxean* 27. 'If, however, it was only a *tertium quid*, some composite essence formed out of the two substances, like the *electrum*, there would be no distinct proofs apparent of either nature.' (That is, of the divine and human natures of Christ.)

not come-to-be, how does it manifest itself in the world? Parmenides asks of us in the *Way of Truth:* 'What beginning are you looking for? What/Origin, what source that might suggest/That it can actually *grow?*' He is insistent that we should never ask such a question of Truth. Yet he knows we must because we are human (he is not insensitive to our needs); and so to ask these questions helps us to draw closer to 'Truth's ardor' as being the 'hidden' aspect of One. He, like Plato after him, recognizes that at some point in our daily lives we must 'lay aside discourse of eternal things', and look to the world for our pleasure in things coming-to-be.[44] These are part of what *is not*, but he knows that we are grounded in *physis* from the moment we are born, and so must partake of the relativity of physical beauty if we are to 'climb the heavenly ladder' at all.

We are lead back to the role of Apollo in Parmenides' evocation of One. Can a god intercede on behalf of men who are in the business of understanding the profound implications of One, the force that contributes to Being and non-being as constituents of the Real, and of reality itself? I believe we can, just as Parmenides called upon the Mistress, Persephone, at the beginning of his poem, to help him. She leads people from Night into the Light, he tells us, from uncomprehending acceptance to a full and deep apprehension of all things. While Apollo, his tutelary deity, provides him with the vital instrument to make such an understanding possible. The bow and lyre

---

44 Plato, *Timaeus* 61c.

contain all the tension of paradox for him; necessarily he cannot resolve such a tension except through music, but at least he can learn to live with its evident merits.

It is for this reason that I wanted to revisit Apollo's presence in Parmenides' life. He does not talk about him in his poem; all we have is a few words on a piece of stone from Elea that tell us of their allegiance. He, like Apollo, is an *ouliades,* a healer. As Apollo uses music to augment the soul, so too does Parmenides make recourse to poetry. They are both in league with One, it seems. As the philosopher remarks, it is an 'empty bolus of unmitigated essence,' this One. Pure *koan* - talk, this. But what it does contain, this 'unmitigated essence', is the talk of a man who has been down into the underworld and met with a goddess. She has taken his hand and brought him forth into the light.

Beauty is the underlining premise of One. Beauty's wide horizon, Plato tells us, transcends all beauties tethered to a world of coming-to-be, to *physis.* It makes it easier now to appreciate what Parmenides is trying to say. He does not want us to get caught up in abstractions, in spite of the difficulties that his poem evokes. He knows the impossibility of trying to articulate the transcendent nature of Being. Nonetheless, he tried to find an image to which he could attach his claims. That image was a ride in a chariot along the Way of Truth, not the way of appearance or falsity.

What must be essential to One that so far I have not explored? With all Parmenides' talk of its self-contained oneness and beauty, and its unity *(henosis)*, I am forced to ask myself why One chooses to impose its presence upon the world, nurturing its plurality for the sake of coming-to-be and being-in-the-world along the way. One does not need to do so as its wholeness is complete. Nothing is added or taken away from One when it decides to effect being. Is this a metaphysical question? Or is it me imposing my own logic upon an imponderable. Parmenides has forced me to take up such a position, nonetheless. His poem has yet to reveal how I must take the path of truth over that of appearance.

From hereon, it is a journey that I must make in order to find out. One is an enduring image of wholeness, of completeness, that simply refuses to recede into the domain of abstraction. Its paradox is ever tantalizing. 'Being alone indescribable,' Proclus writes in his *Hymn to One*, 'It gives rise to all that is spoken... From It all things shine forth; It alone is dependent upon nothing.' Philosophers throughout the ages have wrestled with One's meaning, attaching to it epithets and theogenies to help them make sense of its essence. Why not? If it refuses to reveal itself, except through its emanations in being, it will always clamor for elucidation by succeeding generations of thinkers, just like myself.

VIII

I return to the poem to see whether there is anything that I might have missed. Late in the *Way of Appearance* I read how the goddess Necessity (Ananke) directs the heavenly course of the stars with a 'wand of Love'. And also, how her first-born was Eros – he, the companion of Aphrodite, mistress of seduction and fertility. Buried in Parmenides' cosmological verses detailing the importance of the sun and light to our wellbeing, there lies his perception of an attractive energy that helps to celebrate being-in-he-world. Love is what he alludes to. Between a man and a woman love is embraced, and blood intermingles. He is sure about that. According to Parmenides the world of appearance is founded upon Love. Such is the incomparable energy that One embodies.

In the *Symposium* we encounter a remarkable story about Socrates' meeting with a seer, a priestess from Mantinea known as Diotima, that describes a between-the-two condition known as a *metaxy*. Love in the guise of Eros occupies this position as a go-between in that he mediates between the world of the spirit and that of humankind. Since the gods do not mingle directly with human beings, it rests upon a mediator to perform the task of negotiating the region lying between *apeiron* and *epikeina* - that is, the world of the spirit - through *metaxy*.[45] It is this concept that Parmenides alludes to when he tells us how the goddess Necessity (need) binds all in the heavens as a demonstration of the 'sphere's foundation & limit' with the 'bonds of Limit'. It is the ineluctable law of destiny that he is alluding to, whereby Being must forever be identical with itself.

Plato echoes these sentiments in his own particular way when he expounds what he calls his doctrine of Diotima:

> I was convinced, and in that conviction I tried to bring others to the same creed, and to convince them that, if we are to make this gift our own, Love will help our mortal nature more than all the world. And this is why I say that every man of us should worship the god of Love, and this is why I cultivate and worship all the elements of Love myself, and bid others do the same. And all my life I shall pay the power and the might of Love such homage as I can.[46]

---

[45] Cf. *Symposium* 202e. '... for the divine will not mingle directly with the human, and it is only through the mediation of the spirit-world that man can have any intercourse, whether waking or sleeping, with the gods.'

[46] Ibid. 212b.

Diotima, it seems, acknowledges that to love is to bring forth upon the beautiful, both in body and in soul, a longing not for the beautiful so much as the 'conception and generation that beauty effects'.[47] There is an outcome that beauty makes possible. I try to understand what this assertion means in relationto Parmenides' One. If One is self-sustaining and fulsome, without any need to express itself, where does Love fit in as a generatrix of all the forms within the world? Eros loves; the god Himeros his friend merely desires. Beauty, in effect, is not the product of desire but of love. The reason *for* Beauty is to give birth to love.

Again we find ourselves in the province of Aphrodite who, in the guise of Aphrodite Ourania, is distinct from that of Aphrodite Pandemos as celestial love is to common love. How do we distinguish between the two? I note that Ananke rather than Aphrodite directs the course of the heavens with the wand of love in Parmenides' poem, which suggests a divine love is at work, not one determined by Eros's companion, Himeros - that is, desire. Plato is obviously alluding to two kinds of love, earthly love and Love as an ideal form, when he discusses Diotima's observations about love. This love he and Parmenides talk about is a kind of quintessential ingredient of Being, a divine spark with the power to initiate Beauty, both celestial and physical. Love is a lover of wisdom too.

• • • • • • • • • • • •

47   Ibid. 206c,e.

The Ionian materialist philosophers found a way to explain the transition from One to the Many - *henosis* to *apeiron* - by resorting to their attraction-repulsion theory as represented by Love and Strife. For some reason Parmenides found such an idea too simplistic, perhaps because it was a materialist explanation steeped in the phenomenon of *physis*, and not a metaphysical one which he preferred. Like Plato (or Socrates), he was keen to separate out the workings of One from the activities of Being as an agent of generation in the world. Being stood outside of One, though forever proximate to it. It was an assertion of the unity of essence *and* existence, and was a free act on the part of One. As contradictory as it might sound, the real power of One lay in limitation rather than in diffusion, in *sterisi* or privation rather than in abundance. This is because the eternal beginning of One withdraws its essence from without, and retires into itself.

How does this match up with the idea of Love as the energy of attraction in the world? Did he mean that Love is an independent activity that lies in Being but is not *of* Being? Did he mean that at the heart of our own relationship with love is no more than desire and yearning precipitated by the inner lack that consumes us? Or did he mean that Love can only manifest itself when desire itself is negated? Again as a contradiction, negation is placed before us as a starting-point. One is negated, not because it is the beginning of all number, not because it is itself number, but because it is the negation of number, of multiplicity. All that wishes to grow must first curtail itself. Negation is the first transition from nothing into something.[48]

I believe this is what Parmenides is trying to tell me. He wants me to understand that for all my wish to understand what he means logically, I must, in fact, abandon such an approach. If One has no beginning, then it definitely has no end, either. It is beginningless and endless. For Love to function in such a rarified atmosphere it must partake of another attribute altogether. The answer must lie in the freedom *to* love as the affirmative concept of invoking what might be called an unconditioned eternity, which we can imagine only outside ourselves, outside One. Love is, even as it acts out a contingency in the world as love, a mediator between ourselves and One.

Am I any nearer to understanding Parmenides' belief in love as an attractive force that binds all things in the world? Clearly he struggled with the concept as I do. Where he was travelling as a logician made it difficult for him to turn back on himself and acknowledge the power of Love as a negative, and as a constraint emanating from One via Being itself. The idea contradicted everything he had said about the beginninglessness of One. One didn't 'start' anywhere, so how could Love as an active force 'begin' in itself? It defied logic. He found himself caught up in a paradox of his own making, and he needed to disentangle himself. Plotinus, a late Platonist philosopher from Alexandria, tried to overcome the diffi-

---

48   See Friedrich Schelling, *The Ages of the World* [224].

culties inherent in Love's intent within Being and as an extension to One. He did so by not trying to establish an energy or force at work within One that in turn might allow Love to emerge as an activity within Being, and so flow through to the world at large as the act of love. He did so by elucidating a concept of *thauma*, of wonder that could not be identified by discursive thought. Since One is simple *(haplous)*, non-active and all-encompassing, its metaphysical qualities must somehow be 'transmitted' through an act of wonder. It is well to read what Plotinus wrote in this respect, because he continued to maintain the top-down approach favoured by Parmenides:

> Oh, yes, it is a wonder *(thauma)* how the multiplicity of life came from what is not multiplicity (One), and the multiplicity would not have existed, if what was not multiplicity had not existed before the multiplicity came to be. For the origin is not divided up into the All, because if it were divided up it would destroy the All too; and the All would not any more come into being if the origin did not remain by itself, that is, different from it.[49]

One, in spite of everything, needs to express itself as an Absolute, as an All, and does so by way of wonder. The wonder of the universe is established not by way of what One is, but by negating what multiplicity is. Wonder, too, is another kind of *tertium quid*. Plotinus has adopted what later thinkers called a *via negativa* approach, knowing that only through language and not saying what a thing is can

---

49 Plotinus, *Enneads* III.8.10. 14-19.

the idea of unity in multiplicity be identified. Only through the power of negative argument in philosophy can the idea of a pure existent be posited prior to everyday knowledge becoming possible as a tool.[50] One in unity *(henedos)* becomes a manifestation of multiplicity when it passes through Being into being-in-the-world by way of the activity of wonder *(thauma)*.

I find this argument a rather compelling explanation of how Love works. Neither Parmenides nor Plotinus speak of Love in the context of moving from unity to multiplicity, but it is surely implied. How else could it occur other than through an act of wonder? Love is wondrous, a defiance of the ordinary course of things. It stops, if only for a moment, the flow of being itself. What Parmenides is also implying in his remarks is that One possesses innate motion *(kinesis symphytos)* even though it is always in a state of stasis. The cosmos is 'ordered' into being by One through a free act of Love *(taxis tou kosmou)* which is an act of absolute motion *(autokinesis)*. Being, Rest, and Motion are what might be called a numinal triumphate that exists in One, and give to it its innately moving stability. And Love, finally, gives this triumphate a meaning for us all.

In spite of the fact that One is not and never divided, and always exists as a whole, it nonetheless is able to bring forth, or emanate, from its absoluteness what Plotinus calls a *plethynomenon*, a many-in-itself. The many-in-itself

---

50 Cf. Friedrich Schelling, *The Ages of the World* [243]: 'The original negation is still the mother and nurse of the entire world visible to us.'

is, in its tendency towards multiplicity, an early sign of not-being-the path, we know, Parmenides does not wish us to follow. And yet in *plethynomenon* lies the seeds of wonder in the form of Love! Multiplicity and being are the outcome of love; they germinate in the world as *plethos*, as multiplicity, in such a way that it allows all that is in the world to manifest itself as a form of beauty. Love becomes the agent of beauty in the world. And Parmenides, surely, must have had these thoughts in mind when he penned the *Way of Appearance*. He wanted us to believe in the power of love as a force for renewal and change, even as he suggests the illusory nature of appearance itself, which he saw as a condition of *what isn't*.

Multiplicity, through the act of Love, turns itself inward when it reaches its most extenuating point in matter, thereby connecting it once more to the inwardness of One through the agency of Limit. It never separates itself from One, but remains as a distant determinant of the universe through an ordering, in that the cosmos as we know it is a manifestation of 'ordered beauty' and the inhalation of One as it breathes in the void.[51] Love constitutes an ordered beauty when it resolves opposites, and so finds a way to echo the existence of One, evenwhen it is most distant from One. Love becomes a binding agent *(tertium quid)* that emanates from One, even though One is always in a state of stasis. It draws things together while multiplicity attempts to separate. Without Love we find

---

51   See Plotinus, *Enneads*, VI.1.27-28: 'Thus extension serves as Matter to Beauty since what calls for its ordering is multiplicity.'

ourselves forever immersed in matter, in all the variety and pleasure of physical reality itself, that in turn distances us from One. In Parmenides words we allow ourselves to take the path of *what isn't*. As he says, 'We wander down pathways, hoping/To distance ourselves from the unity of One.'

All this makes me realize how important love is to the creation of the world. It is not just passion or desire, but a wonder. It has, as Plato suggests, celestial connotations. As well, it possesses a generative power and procession as well as multiplicity. Love has the power to turn two into one, reversing the impetus that plurality invokes. Multiplicity, or plurality, is a *posopoios*, that is, a 'quantity-maker' according to Aristotle. It follows that Love is a 'unity-maker' in that it resolves the infinite doubling of things in the world in order to create an image of oneness that reflects the unity of One itself. Love helps to make us perceive One by its infinite capacity to enable us to experience wonder, none other than the wonder of oneness itself.

I believe I am closer to understanding Parmenides' thoughts on Love at last. He attributes to love the labour of birth, fed as it is by 'the embrace of man & woman', but he also sees something more. The physical side of love is but an echo of the absolute of Love which emanates from One. I find this a most satisfying answer to my inquiry. When I started out on this journey into the paradox of diversity within unity as a condition of One, and as a condition of being human, I had no way of knowing how Parmenides might resolve it. What I do know now is that Parmenides was forced to enlist the aid of yet another goddess, this time Necessity (Ananke), in order to explain how love manifests itself in the world. As the goddess that observes Limit, Ananke echoes one of the qualities of One. For all her demands upon us we are nonetheless in her debt.

She makes it possible for us to enter into a relationship with the world as an act of wonder, of necessity.

For all his reliance on logic to make his case for unity-within-diversity, and for the absolute power of One as a remote and unassailable gift to help us understand why we are here as sparks of life in the first place, Parmenides found himself never far away from his beloved gods. They always seem to come to his aid. So far in his poem I have met the Mistress Persephone, Aletheia, Dike, Aphrodite, Ananke, Hemera the goddess of Day, Nyx her counterpart as goddess of Night, Aether the god of Light, as well as the Daughters of the Sun, companions of Apollo, who accompany Parmenides in his chariot. What initially seemed to me a rather dry poem immersed in the style of *via negativa* as a mode of expression, had now allowed other forces to come into play. The voice of the gods had become integral to the poem's evolution as a statement about Being.

The *Way of Truth* is a work of imaginative literature. It is not only a philosophic tract, even if it does appear to be so. We are dealing here with a revelation, not an elegantly composed poem. Some of Parmenides modern detractors argue that he was a poor poet, not realizing that his technique was never going to be sufficient to deal with such an elevated theme as that of the *Way of Truth*. He simply had to unburden himself of a deeply felt belief in *thauma,* in wonder, in order to become the man he became. In doing so he made the transition from that of being a man of knowledge, a seer in the old sense (like Ameinias, his teacher), as well as an *ouliades* or healer as he was known to his fellow Eleatics. He became someone capable of understanding our relationship to One, and the unity of one-and-the-many lying deep in Being, as well as in ourselves. No philosopher or poet before him had ventured into this terrain. He is the first, and his greatness is a signpost pointing the way.

IX

In the *Way of Appearance,* his final attempt to come to terms with the illusory nature of *apeiron,* Parmenides resorts to a touch of irony as he talks about distinction and relativity, telling us that these 'leads away from Truth'. He knows that many might think him mad for overturning accepted cosmological theory in favour of a metaphysical argument for being-in-the-world. Was this not the talk of a Hesiod rather than a Thales? Gods playing havoc with clear and logical thinking also? Irony allows him to counter their criticism; after all, he *knows* their arguments as well as they do. What he wants his critics to understand is that the purely cosmological view cannot be understood simplyby trotting out theories based upon the four elements, as well as adding a little Love and Strife as binding agents.

He tells us that these theories lack depth, because they rely too much upon logic as a tool of comparison. We compare things, we analyze things in the wake of everyday knowledge, because this is what people do. We are practical beings, so we tell ourselves. All of modern science is based upon this fact. To stray from the categorical is to find ourselves in a disorganized state of mind, flailing about among disingenuous realities that we *believe* make sense. If only they did, Parmenides argues. If only what we see and touch possessed the qualities of *what is*. He is adamant, however, because '…what seems to be/ Can never overshadow the claims of Truth.' And Truth lies in the domain of *what is*. There is no getting away from the fact. All the relativities that make up the Many, that is, being-in-the-world, are '… all one resplendent whole,/ A part of the sphere's foundation and limit,' in spite of their fragmentation.

Parmenides is keenly aware of what we are confronted by: whether to give up our unthinking allegiance to being. To do that, we must cease relying upon logic and our various methods of analysis. Such an imperious demand! Has Parmenides the right to ask every one of us to stop thinking the way we do? Most people would agree; the philosopher has overreached himself. He is like a bull in a china shop, or a seer wandering among test tubes in a laboratory. He is trying to overturn *everything*. Will we permit him to contest every premise by which we live? It is a question many of his contemporaries would have asked also, even as young Socrates did when he more or less dismissed Zeno's essay on the nature of *what isn't* as a piece of plagiarism.

The *Way of Appearance* is Parmenides repost to

those who doubted what he had to say. 'Know that the sky, with all its signs,' including the 'pure flame of the sun', are bound together by the goddess, Necessity. This is a metaphysical argument, not a scientific or materialist one. The philosopher has dared to introduce a new way of thinking that stands outside the older mythological mode, as well as any new scientific explanations espoused by his Ionian contemporaries about the four elements. Parmenides wanted us to think differently, to embark upon a thought-process that included the metaphysical. He, unlike any before him, understood that if one really wishes to travel the Way *(hodos)*, then we must accept that 'apprehending [with thinking] and being are one and the same.' Yet what lies *outside* thinking and being opens up a whole new dimension to reality for the very first time.

This is the biggest challenge posed by Parmenides' poem. He wants us to think outside the box of logic. His One transcends number and presents us with the emptiness of naught, the all transcendent O, as an image that contains within its sphericity as a metaphysical construct *more* than being and the cosmos. In contrast, his Ionian counterparts were happy to bring things down to earth in their theories and explanations. The four elements and the accompanying energies of attraction and repulsion seemed to them sufficient enough. Why should one want to go further, descend ever deeper into the reality of Being in an attempt to look for answers? Homer hadn't, nor had Thales, even though the latter maintained the immortality of the soul as a physical reality - which was, in a sense, partly a metaphysical argument.[52] Parmenides' sphere embodied a much more complex explanation about the relationship between Being and being, *what is* and *what isn't,* which was entirely *un*physical.

The answer lay in his understanding of limit. The inordinately composed and unfathomable nature of One is empowered by Limit. What strikes me as soremarkable about such a statement is the fact that the 'emptiness' of One is somehow 'filled' by the concept of limitation. It is hard to comprehend what such a statement means. We are used to things - a cup, for example - being empty or full, even half-full. Substance, in this case water, occupies a particular space. This is a thoroughly naturalistic argument. We can see such a reality with our own eyes because it is physical, and know it to be a fact. But what Parmenides is suggesting is that this practical explanation is *only half the story.*

He truly believes that the predominant energy at work within us is one of Intellect. It is Intellect or Mind *(Nous)* that 'moves the *whole body'* to think within us. Does he also mean 'soul' in this case? Possibly. He does inform us that 'thought is regal/The very substance of our mortal

· · · · · · · · · · · · ·

52   See Aristotle: 'Thales, too, to judge from what is recorded of his views, seems to suppose that the soul is in a sense the cause of movement, since he says that a stone [magnet, or lodestone] has a soul because it causes movement to iron' *(De An.* 405a 20-22); also, 'Some think that the soul pervades the whole universe, whence perhaps came Thales's view that everything is full of gods.' *(De An.* 411a 7-8). Soul gives all bodies their determination and rational configuration, which in turn reaches into every aspect of the physical world. According to Plato, it is the lowest rational power shining in from the All Soul.

coils.' Is soul regal, then? Again, possibly. He asks us to regard thinking and intellect as embodying wisdom. So that the role of intellect is not just to think, but to acknowledge contradiction as an important method for comprehending the universe. We should not accept what we see, or believe what we know, to be the sum total of things. Intellect is the chariot upon which we must travel if we are to reach our final destination along the Way.

I have always been fascinated by Parmenides description of his chariot's spinning wheels emitting the sound of a panpipe. On the surface it suggests no more than a squealing sound, the result of axles heated by excessive friction. Or does it have another meaning to do with the ritual use of sound as a method for preparing the transition from the world we know into that of the spirit? A panpipe was known as a *syrinx*, itself a reference to the nymph Syrinx who Pan pursued into a river where she was transformed into a reed in order to escape his avid affections. The sound *(syrigmos)* that she made, haunting and mournful as it is, was the sound of the reed pipe when Pan blew across its opening, seeking out Syrinx.

For a chariot's wheels to be compared to the sound of a panpipe makes me wonder what Parmenides had in mind.[53] If the sound of a panpipe is an indication of a

....

53   Parmenides' journey by chariot through the Gates of Light and Night are echoed in the Kaushitika Upanishad: 'As a man riding in a chariot looks down on two chariot-wheels on either side, so does he on either side look down in day and night, deeds good and evil, and all dualities.' (Note: See Ch. X for further elaboration on the links between Parmenides' thought and Eastern philosophy).

transition from one state to another, then Parmenides is asking us to make such a transition ourselves. As a call for silence, the syrinx enunciates the sound of creation in the form of the 'harmony of the spheres' said to have been made popular by Pythagoras, who believed that the universe actually *sings*.[54] If this is so, if Parmenides is alluding to his Pythagorean teachers and their knowledge of harmonics as those offering an 'opening' into the spiritual world, then one can understand the significance of the chariot making a noise like a panpipe. It wants us to move beyond the world we are familiar with, the world of *physis*, into the domain of One.[55]

When Parmenides extolls the realm of being as a condition of *what isn't* in his *Way of Appearance*, I begin to realize that he is merely reiterating his belief in One as the overarching principle of Being, a predication of

- - - - - - - - - - - - -

54 See Pliny the Elder, *Natural History* (II. 17.20): '... occasionally Pythagoras draws on the theory of music, and designates the distance between the Earth and the Moon as a whole tone, that between the Moon and Mercury as a semitone the seven tones thus producing the diapason, *i.e.* a universal harmony'.
Again, in Simplicius, *Commentary on the Second Book of the Treatise of Aristotle On the Heavens*: '... that a harmonic sound was produced from the motion of the celestial bodies, and they scientifically collected them from the analogy of their intervals.' (quoted by Iamblichus)
Also, Hyppolytus, *Refut.* 1, 2, 2. '[Pythagoras] was the first to reduce the motion of the seven heavenly bodies to rhythm and song'.

55 The Aborigines of Australia, when they perform sacred rituals, often resort to the use of a bullroarer prior to the enactment of rites. Its mournful sound conjures up an otherworldly effect, some say of the Dreaming spirits speaking to the participants. Having experienced such an event myself, I know that the sound of the bullroarer marks a break with the mundane world.

isness imbedded in *what is*. As well, depending on how much 'light or darkness exists/In our bodies,' that is, how much we allow our lives to be determined by goodness, so do we embody wisdom, that mysterious ingredient possessed by Being alone. Wisdom, at least according to Iamblichus, is a 'certain science which is conversant with the first beautiful objects,' none other than those ideal forms of Plato.[56] We now find ourselves thrown back into the *Way of Truth* once more by the philosopher in his bid to affirm the eternal reality of One. Parmenides will not let us off the hook: we must embrace *what is* as the only framework for living a reasonable life.

The Many, that is *Physis* in its multiplicity, is determined by number, and Parmenides would have more than likely known this fact through his contact with Pythagoreans, who had made a science of them. Though he does not mention number in his poem, it is implicit when he talks about the 'simple properties of existence'. The world of being is constructed by number. 'As Hypasus said, all those destined to a quinqeunnial silence [the adepts or *homacoi*] call number the judicial instrument of the maker of the universe, and the first paradigm of mundane fabrications.'[57] Parmenides knows that number is essential to existence; it defines the nature of limit within the domain of the unlimited. Without the implicit order as embodied in number, the world would fragment

---

56   Ibid. *Nat. Hist.* Ch. XII.

57   Iamblichus, *Life of Pythagoras*. Ch. XXVIII. Also, 'The essence of God is number.'

into a chaotic mass. One is the final arbiter of number. Its naughtness precipitates number by way of an 'emanation' of its innermost self. Number is made manifest through the mystery of One.

If number is a conterminous factor within One, then its manifestation in the concept of mathematics is one of the wonders of metaphysics. Duality is an act of *apostasis*, denoting a becoming and a manifestation of being itself. It is said that Pythagoras himself studied the science of numbers while in Egypt, which must have influence Parmenides in some way. Unity 'moves' into being andbecomes manifold by way of numbers.

Plotinus tells us that multiplicity is a falling away from Unity, and infinity (limitlessness) being a complete departure from it, is a giving birth to innumerable multiplicities. He further tells is that 'unlimit' is an evil.[58] Number precipitates a flowing out of self-centredness towards dissipation and a state of extension. While Plotinus might view this as an 'evil', I do not believe that Parmenides does so. He would argue that self-imitation, a condition of One, opens the way towards synthesis, a miracle in its own right.

'Since a thing must feel its exile, its sundrance from essence', that is how Plotinus terms it. In feeling one's exile, however, one inevitably feels a desire notto continue

- - - - - - - - - - - -

58 See *Enneads*, 6.1. It should be noted that in Greek the word for 'evil' is derived from 'to miss the mark' as in archery. It also means 'to err'. The connotations that Christian theology places upon the word are entirely absent.

in an outwardly moving direction towards frustration or compulsion (multiplicity or extension), because One's sole desire is to return to a state of unity. He further tells us that Beauty is the shield that parries multiplicity and magnitude. Beauty holds us ever beholden to Limit. As well, Beauty calls for the ordering of multiplicity. It is for this reason that we love art; it acts within limits to define beauty.

For Parmenides, just as it is for Plotinus, there is no otherness derived from a falling away from One; but rather, an otherness that is derived from One. It is not a deteriorating act for him so much as an innate motion *towards* multiplicity. Things come into existent for a particular reason. Firstly, because they have no entity in One except as an aspect of Unity. And secondly, because when they emerge from Being, they are already destined to become the Many. Their otherness is a manifestation of being, transitory at best, but at least a form of multiplicity that ensures the continued existence of the universe.

Desire becomes the activating force that urges all things into a state of fragmentation; and yet, by a miracle, desire *(himeros)* also turns multiplicity inward again in the direction of its origin in One. This desire is that of *orexis*, of caring and longing. Animals long and care for their world, since it is not an object for them. Rather, the world is encountered in the mode of an uplifting, a love for it for its own sake. Desire makes possible a moving-toward or away from something, and so becomes a fundamental mode of being. The cycle is everfulfilling, at least according to Parmenides.[59]

One is not so much some abstract sphere that embodies unity as an unapproachable entity. While it seems that way, given that the philosopher is reluctant to give more details as to its essence, we must nonetheless assume that One 'contains' something, even if it is a tendency towards instantation. Limit tends towards the Unlimited when it manifests itself in Being, that 'place' where absolutes are reformulated for their entry into being *(physis)* in the guise of multiplicity, the unlimited. How Parmenides explains such a phenomenon is by resorting to the isness of things in Being, as ideal forms, existing in a prior state before they manifest themselves in being, again as *physis*. This is a more familiar and satisfying way of expressing One, not as some remote construct, but as what Parmenides views as a wholeness, a *hypophysikon phos* or supernatural light.

How I deal with this fact is to put aside my confusion so that I might embrace the unrelenting logic of his arguments as being no more than the superstructure of a far more subtle entity, which he is trying to explain. They

- - - - - - - - - - - - -
> 59 An idea which is reminiscent of Nietzsche's rather bleak revelation of the Eternal Return: 'What, if some day or night a demon were to steal after you into your loneliest loneliness and say to you: 'This life as you now live it and have lived it, you will have to live once more and innumerable times more' ... Would you not throw yourself down and gnash your teeth and curse the demon who spoke thus? Or have you once experienced a tremendous moment when you would have answered him: 'You are a god and never have I heard anything more divine." *(The Gay Science)*

supply the scaffold to which the 'form' of One clings. I cannot explain such a formulation, nor can Parmenides; it simply is. So long as I am unable to picture its reality except as a sphere, then I am half way towards understanding the pure metaphysicality of One. This leaves me with the opportunity to indulge in an act of *thauma*, of wonder. I have no other way of expressing what I feel in the presence of One. One is where eternal images are created, each articulated by the perfection of Number, so that in being and multiplicity they remain a distant echo of Unity as number in the world.

For Parmenides only One *is*. Everything else *isn't*. I recognize that he is not calling into question the contingent reality of being-in-the-world: that he readily accepts as a part of the joy and suffering of life. He is not asking us to turn our backs on matter either, as if it were some kind of dark abysm that might destroy us; but rather, he wants us to understand our relationship to it as a temporary condition *of being*. He expressed such a thought in the last lines of his poem:

> Mark well, all this is mere opinion
> That formulates and grows, then fades away
> As mature thought intervenes. And yet
> At some point each was given a name
> As if it partook of the very bliss of being.

Here we have it. When we think outside the box of the everyday, we will have to, at some stage, recognize that in attaching names to things, that we are merely creating a construct in which we can live and function. This is not Being or One. It is an armrest, a comfort, that makes life bearable.

So here I am, on the brink of some new revelation that the poem has so farnot revealed. Why do I say this? After all, it has talked to me about unity and multiplicity. It has talked to me about love. It has even talked to me about the journey each of us must make if we wish to find meaning in our personal life. It has spoken about those error-filled ways that lead nowhere at all, except into that pool of suffering into which many of us have plunged.

Parmenides has alerted me to what illusion really means. I am better equipped to deal with the limitations of rational thought when faced with the apogee known as intuitional knowledge. He does not talk about that, but he has it in mind. Why would he confront us with so much contradiction, so much frustration about the nature of Limit and its diffusion throughout being if he did not acknowledge the existence of a paradox, of a *creative* paradox? Because he knows, as few before him had done, that lying below the surface of contradiction and limitation is the prospect of being swept up into the 'very bliss of being', as he so wisely tells us. Contradiction is life's mainspring and core.

'Shining by night with borrowed light/Does the moon wander about the earth/Always indebted to the moon's rays.' Here is his paean to the miracle of the cosmos, to the world, to life. Love-seed, too, blends in man and woman to create an echo of One in being.[60] We live in this reality, as Parmenides did in Elea. He, a legislator and philosopher of the city, nonetheless sought to find an answer to the great issue of Being and being, One and Many, for himself. I admire him for his pertinacity, his *tenacity*.

Along with his Pythagorean antecedents he discovered in the idea of multiplicity the very basis for the composition of the universe. Like Plotinus after him, he observed in the figure of the sphere a perfect configuration of One, that in its homogeneity and self-identity, reflected his belief in Limit as the defining agency of Being. Men had talked about these ideas before him, but none had shown the clarity of thought to write them down in the form of a poem.

When he goes on to write in his poem about the physical aspects of conception as it relates to men and women, indeed to all creatures, we get the sense that he is trying to describe how the unlimited manifests itself as traits in individual character. He is merely reiterating facts that previous thinkers had articulated with regard to the way conception works. We may think them wrong, but this is not the point. How much darkness or light that exists in a person is determined by the 'accident' of conception in the womb, which for Parmenides is more

---

60 See Appendix 1

important than any gynecological explanation.[61]

He sees this as yet another example of the actions of Eros generating diversity in the world, and the transient nature of physical reality itself. Is this not a wonder? He wants us to know that a woman's womb is a place where One resides as an inchoate force working with the help of number and the unlimited to invoke identity and difference. It is an echo of Being in being, a demonstration of *hypophysikon phos* at work in the human body. In spite of the provisional nature of being-in-the-world, we are always linked to the eternal reality of One.

His doctrine of 'twin seeds,' however, does make a good deal of sense. The idea that one might be born with a predominance of 'darkness' in one character goes a long way to explaining why some of us are moody, morose, given to fits of melancholy and even madness. It also intimates as to why evil might exist in the world. If we take Parmenides at his word, then evil is a demonstration of darkness over that of light. It is a concept that we can perfectly understand.

What we might not wish to accept is the degree of determinism that misdirected semen in the womb contributes to the level of darkness in our character. And yet, is not such an explanation a help towards understanding how multiplicity works in the world, even if it

- - - - - - - - - - - - -

61 The Aborigines of Australia also believe that biological conception plays a less important part in the true act of conceiving. This act occurs when a father 'dreams' his future progeny while walking through a particular landscape in the bush. When the child is later born, that piece of country become his or her totemic home. Conception is thus an act of metaphysical insemination.

does not conform to the physiological knowledge that we have come to accept? The metaphor of a wombin turmoil before birth might well be a manifestation of the confusion and disjointedness of life as we know it.

Parmenides is telling us that the 'unmixed fire' of One does offer to us its 'portion of light'. Though we can never dispense entirely with the impermanence of our physical condition in the form of 'iron's configurations' or the 'miracle of the moon', we nonetheless partake of something special when we enter this world. That is not deterministic because it *is* a miracle. Parmenides tells us, that in spite of our flaws, we are blessed with a 'whole body' through which we think and act. There is no hiatus here; rather, a way of clawing back the light in our character from any darkness that we might assume there to be. Such is the challenge of life: to move towards Being in being, to yearn for the aeternality and self-identity of One even as we enjoy the multiplicity of being itself.

We must always keep in mind that Parmenides' One is not material but a metaphysical construct. He made it possible for us to think metaphysically about the Unknowable by giving us a form *(morphai)* to help us think in a non-material way about Being. This was his great contribution to the way we think outside of the realm of *physis*. Later philosophers such as Aristotle, Theophrastus, and Eudemus misinterpreted his ideas to mean that One enjoyed physical properties, which it does not. In part this was because they were too enamoured by the Ionian philosophers belief in the material nature of reality.

Plato also suggested that One, though a mystery (as Aristotle too acknowledged) represented a 'unity of all things', which again suggested its embodiment as a physical reality. The path that the west subsequently took from this point on led us to think of Being as a physical reality only. Modern science is based upon such a premise. It was left to later philosophers such as Plotinus and Porphyry to re-affirm the metaphysical nature of One – and Parmenides' vision - for a world starved of spiritual sustenance. For them, as for Parmenides, One is indivisible, and so not able to be accessed by any ordinary thinking.

Parmenides represents one of the great spiritual thinkers of all time. Though he might have counted himself a poet or a philosopher first, his thought tells us much more about ourselves and our penchant for illusion as a mode of life than it does about the unfathomable nature of One, as powerful as this is. In this sense he is an *ouliades* who has the capacity to heal our beleaguered spirit. He teaches us the importance of remaining true to Being as the only way *to* live. Other thinkers since him have told us that this is the only true way – men and women such as Francis of Assisi, John of the Cross, Terese of Avila, John of Ruusbroec, and in our own time Edith Stein and Simone Weil, to name but a few. Each of these spirituals might count him or herself as worthy disciples of Parmenides if they had known of his One as the supreme metaphysical edifice that it is. Perhaps they did.

X

Some scholars argue that Parmenides' understanding of reality was far too rigid to stand up to critical analysis. He had created a monster in the realm of thought, a creature that ate away at the very substance of the everyday world to the point where it no longer existed, except as an illusion. The second part of his poem was seen as an attempt to justify the existence of a *diakosmos*. That is, a world-order which does not exist other than an as aspect of change. The naming of opposites he regarded as a mere habit of thought that made it easy for us *not* to explore One as the primordial essence of Being because it merely gave us a platform for dialectic. As far as he was concerned, to think meaningfully about something that did not exist – namely, the world as we know it - was not to invoke knowledge as such, but the *illusion* of knowledge.

No wonder so many people recoiled from his vision. The idea that the natural world did not exist except as an elaborate illusion was hard to accept, even though it is part of the Vedantic and Buddhism traditions. Commentators argued that Parmenides had overreached himself, that he had allowed his extreme rationalism to overwhelm his common sense. How can we dismiss the world? It doesn't make sense at all. No one in his right mind wants to maintain that real existence is little more than a column of smoke! Yet this is precisely what Parmenides wants us to recognize: that true knowledge is not achieved through the enactment of our senses. Such knowledge is no more than skin-deep, and a superficial analysis of being. Real knowledge, the knowledge that is not understood by our discursive intellect or by any prescribed conventions of language, which are rudimentary at best, can only be accessed by a full and unmitigated understanding of One *outside language*.

Change and illusion are at the heart of his thinking about how we view our place in the world. It is a way of thinking familiar to those who understand the Vedanta or the teachings of the Buddha with their doctrine of non-duality (*advaita-vada*). The Upanishads place particular emphasis upon the idea of Maya, of illusion, but it is not illusion as we know it. Maya really means 'not as it seems' (ie. Parmenides' 'appearance' or 'opinion'), that our senses are mistaken whenever they apprehend the world. Knowledge of Maya is not true knowledge, but knowledge distorted by our individual ego. It is this kind of knowledge of the material world that Parmenides wants us to accept as illusory. It is not the eternal, unchanging knowledge of One, but the temporary and changing knowledge of *physis* – or, as the Vedanta calls it, *prakrti,* a condition of the temporary and changing material world, which is nature itself.

Parmenides, for all his rationalism, wants us to think mystically when we approach One. His argument for doing so is closer to the voice of the Upanishads than he is to his friends among the Ionian philosophers, wedded as they are to atomism and the material universe. One and Brahman are the same in this context. In the Maitri Upanishad we read an almost exact description of Parmenides' One:

> In the beginning all was Brahman, ONE and infinite. He is beyond the north and south, east and west, and beyond what is above and below. His infinity is everywhere. In him there is nothing above, nor across, nor below; his spirit is immeasurable, inapprehensible, never-born, beyond reasoning, beyond thought. His vastness is the vastness of space.
>
> ... There is something beyond our mind which abides in silence within our mind. It is the supreme mystery beyond thought. Let one's mind and one's subtle body rest upon that, and not rest on anything else.[62]

The further I venture into the lore of the Upanishads, the nearer I come to understanding what Parmenides did not say explicitly in his great poem. When he writes 'Mighty chains bind it to its unbeginning/And to its

---
62 *The Upanishads.* Maitri Upanishad, 6.17 and 6.19.

unceasing since birth & death/Have been driven to a far place by Truth...' he is alerting me to the imponderable nature of One, as well as Its capacity to create the illusory world of being itself. Withdrawing from the world of the here-and-now is to re-establish one's connection to Truth. The Upanishads would argue that such an event only happens when we dream: that in dreams we carry the material of everyday events and experiences to a place where they are subjected to the radiance of Brahman. When we wake up we are once more in the realm of freedom, if only for a moment.

The Upanishads also tell us that One is both distant yet approachable, something that Parmenides does not quite acknowledge. His One has all the ingredients of a Penelope who refuses every suitor's hand. One, or Brahman, is more familial to the Eastern mind than it was to his. It tolerates delusion as a basis for being-in-the-world because it makes plurality, multiplicity, and beauty the hallmarks of such an existence. Parmenides wanted his One to be utterly unapproachable, even though he accepted that it *had* to engage in manifestation if the world was to be.

Parmenides wanted to emphasize a condition that the Upanishads also acknowledged: that the mind, when it is subject to the world, is forever in a state of bondage. To be free of bondage requires a concerted act of going beyond desire. He would have been happy to accept Maitri Upanishad's premise, however, that 'If men thought of God as much as they thought about the world, who would not attain to liberation?'[63]

Nonetheless, Parmenides believed in the power of Unity to cleanse the senses of their delusions. Naming things is a pathway to disunity, he knew, because in doing so we exclude the possibility of attaining to a supreme silence. Words make it impossible to experience silence, for they are in league with the relativisation of the world, except when they are sacralized as in the word AUM, which is the 'resonance' of One. *Perusha,* or the all-pervading nature of Brahman, lies beyond definitions, beyond language, beyond all concepts, so we are told. Its form is not in the field of vision, just as Parmenides' One is not. Though it can be 'seen' as such by a pure heart, and by a mind whose thoughts are pure, this they both agree upon. It is the law of One as it is of Brahman.

Parmenides is pleading with us to break with our modern conception that the world is founded upon the so-called laws of nature. He is asking us to acknowledge that there is a limit as to how we explain things in the world. This is difficult for those of us who are accustomed to accepting the conclusions of science as the basis for all knowledge. According to him, the opinions that we establish as fact are always subject to the contingencies of change and error.

They simply '… fade away/As mature thought intervenes.' Yet at some point, he tells us, they were 'given a name,' as if in naming them they 'partook of the very bliss of being.' Such are the delusions of language and of

---

63   Ibid. 6.24

our senses, Parmenides insists. Yet it can equally be said that factual knowledge, while not based upon a secure foundation, can *grow* if it is subject to discussion and new ideas.

Change is a condition of disunity-within-unity, he seems to be telling us. The isness of One reveals itself in this unique way. What sees variety and not unity wanders on from death to death, the Upanishads say. Therefore we must embrace change not as a periodicity, but as a condition of gradual ensoulment. It is attached to time in a way that makes motion its helpmate. Parmenides insists that we must come to terms with these realities if we want to understand the nature of One.

Change, illusion, time, and motion are the horses hauling his chariot through the Gates of Night and Light. They are the energy and power of creation asserting itself as magnitude in the world of being. They are the power, also, of ours senses. We are told in the Upanishads that if these horses are well-reined, then our sense are under control. 'Know the Atman as Lord of the chariot, the body as the chariot itself. Know that reason is the charioteer; and the mind indeed is the reins'.[64]

In essence, Parmenides wants to remind us that there is no possibility of invariants existing outside One. For them to exist outside One would eliminate change as an aspect of motion. Change (or transition) is predicated upon the idea of a thing not being itself at some point in time, even if it does not depart from its essential constit-

- - - - - - - - - - - -
64   Ibid. *Katha Upanishad,* Part 3.

uent. Some might argue that a thing is not a thing as such, but a process, since it is always undergoing change.

A leaf turning brown, for example, is a representation of change; it travels in time towards its brownness. We are accustomed to seeing a green leaf and a brown one as being essentially the same; they partake of leafiness, hence our illusion. But for Parmenides they are not the same. A decrepitation has occurred, a state of decay has intervened. The form or suchness of the green leaf has been lost. Such a condition embodies his argument of *what isn't,* the very condition that he tells us to beware of as the manifestation of an aeternal event. Life-forms and their changing nature are thus an *attenuation* of One, and therefore not truly of *what is* since they partake of change.

It occurs to me that Parmenides might like me to consider a state of what I call *metaphysis* as a way of engaging with the world. Without such a word, it makes it difficult to deal with what he might desire of me. To live in a state of *metaphysis* is to always think metaphysically about the world. Certain rare people do, of course, although they likely call themselves mystics in deference to their holistic views. Be that as it may: I am happy to grapple with a new way of thinking that might enhance how I alternate between the unity of One and the multiplicity of being-in-the-world, if it helps me to better understand.

Metaphysis as a state relies on the realization of a certain kind of knowledge that cannot be achieved by reasoning alone. Since there is only one reality, namely the reality of One, to know that reality demands that I choose to *inhabit truth*. Though change might be paradoxical and in part causal, truth is not. Like One, Truth is. 'Where I begin is all One to me, & I will/Return again & again to this refrain,' he tells us. While time and motion do not exist in One, because One is full and not empty and so cannot move, therefore the nature of One *as an indivisible* is presented to me more or less as a *fait accompli*. It follows that to achieve a state of *metaphysis*, I must enter into a motionless state. This is to say that I have entered into the fullness of One through an act of contemplation.

I am reminded of some words by the Spanish mystic, Peter of Alcantara, a friend of Saint Teresa of Avila:

> In meditation we consider carefully divine things, and we pass from one to another, so that the heart may feel love. It is as though we should strike a flint to draw a spark of fire.
>
> In contemplation the spark is struck: the love we were seeking is here. The soul enjoys silence and peace, not by many reasonings, but by simply contemplating the Truth.

In a state of *metaphysis*, when one has gone beyond the physical domain of knowing and determining, such an act of contemplation yields a particular offering. The Kaushitaki Upanishad informs us that in order to achieve this state a person must cease speaking, and concentrate on breathing only. One must sacrifice speech to breath if one is to remain awake rather than asleep. [65] Silence is the primary ingredient of *metaphysis* as we know from the principle of *hesychia* practiced in ancient Greece; it allows, metaphorically at least, for a cessation of a breathing-in and out of the universe that Parmenides would have understood from his contemporaries as a basis for the existence of that universe. The world is stilled. One becomes an act of instilment. When the fire burns, so does Brahman shine.

It is no accident that many of the older Upanishads were written around the same time as Parmenides' *Way of Truth*, and may have influenced him in an indirect way through his family connections in Iona.[66] They represent a call to wisdom as a counter to the pressures of the everyday. Parmenides' plea for men to contemplate One, as distinct from the illusions of *apeiron*, present us with a similar insight. Surrounded as we are by time and change, multiplicity and decay, the idea of an absolute Truth existing outside the relative and contingent is of some comfort. It means that we do not have to immerse ourselves in the everyday in order to discover our own immortality. *What is* is eternal, and so immortal. When isness is perceived of as an ontological reality as Parmenides suggests, then do we begin to embrace the prospect of One as a pure invariant. The Upanishads inform us in a similar vein: 'This in

- - - - - - - - - - - - -

65 *Kaushitaki Upanishad*, 2.5

66 See W.L. West, *Early Greek Philosophy and the Orient*. (p. 226): 'His father and teachers may have been among the original Phocaean founders of Elea, bringing minds fresh from Ionia.'

truth is That'.

It is important to appreciate that parallels do exist across cultures. Parmenides does not stand alone as a thinker. Though his contemporaries might have been aghast at his monistic bias, he would have found a sympathetic ear in India. There, the concept of One found its garb in Brahman, Love or Eros in the clothing of Shiva, *Apeiron* in the patched cloth of Maya. The depth of images in Hindu thought is more apparent than it was for Parmenides. He grappled with abstract forms because he was afraid of slipping back into the domain of mythos, which he knew had already lost its power to inform metaphysics. Somehow he felt the need to be more rigorous in his thinking, more rational in his bid to place One on the throne of intellect as a perfect embodiment of aeternality and Truth.

We cannot argue with him for taking such a course, even if he might have wishedfor Apollo to come to his aid. Parmenides was a metaphysical rationalist who sought to extricate Greek philosophy from its mythological origins and its materialist tendencies. In a sense, he was thrown out of his myth.

If we are to accept his understanding of One as an absolute entity, we must also accept it as possessing a causal effect. While he might have denied the possibility of change, except as a micro-event in the conduct of being (a green leaf becoming a brown one), it does not mean that change had been eliminated from his purview in the ordinary sense. He was simply arguing for the absoluteness of One and of Being as the final arbiter of existence. For him, the act of becoming was derived from sense perception only, faulty at best, that it lies within the domain of world-process. All he was saying is that 'certain truth' lies within One, and is beyond the reach of man. It is a constituent of divine knowledge just as it was for his friend Xenophanes, who advised him early in his career when they were both residents of Elea.

Is it possible to engage with such a man, remarkable as he seems? I sense that Parmenides lived two lives – one as a public figure and *ouliades* in the service of his community, the other as a thinker deeply committed to understanding the nature of the universe. The Goddess had granted him a revelation, and he felt impelled to make it his own. His grave demeanor towards the end of his life, as commented upon by Socrates when they first met, is a reflection of the distance he had travelled away from common opinion, or indeed the thought of many of his contemporaries. Here was a man who had conversed with others of like mind in Magna Grecia as a young man, men such as Ameinias and Xenophanes, and learnt from them all that they knew from their teachers. Above all, what he learnt was that the universe was a mysterious phenomenon that needed to be addressed in a new language, both cosmologically and metaphysically, if it were to be understood. He chose the language of poetry.

XI

How, then, do I make Parmenides a part of my own life? It is a question that I have long asked of myself. We do not readily think of philosophers as spiritual guides. They seem so remote from us, living as they do as half-gods in the shade of some Stoa. Who reads Plato or Plotinus these days other than the occasional academic? Very few of us, if the truth be known. We find the sheer power of their intellects to be utterly daunting, leaving little room for ordinary life to make its appearance. We see them as relics of the past, and representatives of an old style of thinking that has no bearing on our everyday lives. To enter Parmenides world as I have done in these pages might be considered an exercise in nostalgia: that I am yearning to find some meaning in my life which older, outmoded theologies with their emphasis upon faith, no longer offer.

What strikes me about Parmenides and his friends is that they lived full lives in the world. They did not become recluses, not even Pythagoras. Through the strength of their intellects they found a way to affirm existence as both a real and contingent thing, even as they made inquiries into what the Absolute might look like. They lived double lives. One life that *is,* and another life that was *less.* I don't mean this observation as a criticism. Nor do they. They simply asked themselves primary questions while they went about their business each day. What is time, duration, unity, multiplicity, motion, space, the heavens, the power of number, death, love, strife, life as a man or as a god, they asked themselves? Are these questions that any of us should ask, since no clear answer can ever be found? Yet Parmenides and his friends did inquire of them because they were never satisfied with what had been told to them by their poets and mytho-graphers.

    The French philosopher, Pierre Hadot, wrote that philosophy is a method for achieving independence and inner freedom.[67] If this is not a genuine aspiration for every one of us today, than I cannot imagine what alternative life one could lead. It is for this reason that I believe it is important to interrogate men such as Parmenides, and see whether they are able to say something to me that is still relevant. The man struggled to express what he thought, and his thought sounds obscure to a modern ear. But this does not mean that what he wrote in his poem, the *Way of Truth,* is not an enduring legacy. As I have remarked earlier, his poem is one that changed the way

- - - - - - - - - - - - -

67   Pierre Hadot, *Philosophy as a Way of Life.*

we think about everything we hold dear. It is the poem that changed the world.

To be in the company of such a man is to know how important it is to ask questions of myself. Why do I question the value of life? Why do I ask myself whether my life is of any significance? Is thinking an activity of the privileged only? I could go on and on, testing what are ageless verities uttered by men like Parmenides in relation to my own self-centeredness, as well as his desire to find a meaning in life. I could tell myself that it really doesn't matter whether One is, or whether Limit and Number might be the foundation of the entire cosmos. Such thoughts do not put a meal on the table or make me any happier. Or do they? I had never thought about how impoverished my life might have become in the absence of those 'unshakable records' that Schelling suggests are the only sure ground upon which we should stand if we wish to reach a state of autarchy, of inner calm.

All matter is spiritual in the broad sense, so that when Parmenides derides *physis* as being steeped in the unlimited, the contingent, and the ever-changing, he is not really being as dismissive as he sounds. He knows that the miraculous transition from One to Being to Intellect, and finally to being in the physical sense, this is not a denigration of ordinary existence. Far from it. He knows that we have to live in the world, to deal with everyday reality and to manipulate facts whenever the need arises. His aim is not to disparage the illusory nature of existence, either. However, he does expect us to *know* that there is a difference between what may be absolute and what is contingent, illusory. If we go about our daily lives believing in what our senses tell us all the time, at the cost of questioning their claim upon the truth of things, then we are liable to fall into the trap of believing that the individual 'I' in us is actually real.

Whenever I have spent time among indigenous peoples in Borneo forests or the deserts of Australia, I have always felt that I was close to the Beginning. I think this is what Parmenides wants me to remember: the Beginning is a primordial moment that stands outside time, and yet remains ever-present in the minds and hearts of men. It is, in its own way, a quintessential One which becomes Many in the course of entering time. He is telling me to hold back on a ready acceptance of the seductive appearance of the world, which is no more than a legacy of habitual actions, in order to contemplate a more substantial truth. And what is this truth? That we live in a plenum where stillness and motion cohabit. While we are drawn into action, we must never forget how important it is to retreat into stillness, into a state of *hesychia*.

Parmenides' One is a distant echo of that stillness. Through stillness it is possible to reframe the whole of our lives, and the whole of existence. The world is nurtured and thrives on our stillness. It does not enjoy agitation, even though there is so much of it around. Natural catastophes are grounded in self-movement, which is a condition of agitation. What the earth seeks, as we all do, is to find itself in a state of eternal rapture, even though we know this not to be feasible. As One outwardly turns towards being-in-the-world, so do we turn inward in the hope of being received back into One. A complementarity is achieved: the world exists so that One might celebrate its existence. The world as we know it is none other than a smile on the face of One. Without the world, One has no reason to exist. It is inconceivable.

I take comfort in this knowledge. For the first time I understand what it means to live within the domain of Limit, of limitation *(periorismos)*. It is the carapace over Parmenides' bright sphere, and the receptacle that 'contains' the definite. Outside this sphere all is indefinite, diffused, tending towards magnitude and the inordinate. That is our world. We live among magnitudes, ever-growing, ever-diminishing, full of change, fluid, a part of the uneasy flow of things as they are. Nor can we help ourselves from embracing this fulsome yet transitory existence. Parmenides know this fact well enough, even as he wants us to have a care for the value of limitation in our lives. *Periorismos* is a spiritual condition as far as he is concerned. It blossoms like a flower in the soil of our constraint.

He speaks of Love also, a state he sees as a kind of luminous attraction ever at work in being. It is, however, more than the attraction of love as we know it. That love is psychological, and represents no more than a distant echo of Love as a constituent of Being. Parmenides' Love may wield a wand, but this is only because he delights in metaphor. His Love is stripped of all such decoration; but this does not mean, that as a powerful and enduring force of attraction, it is not allowed to participate in the creation of the world.

His Love, rather, is metaphysical: it strives to inform the ordinary with *thambos*, the sheer dazzle of existence. In the presence of *thambos* we find ourselves observing one-hundred little figures saluting the sun, dazzled by it, as men and women who are watching it happen while standing on a high summit. Love, at least from Parmenides' point of view, is to stand on a summit and observe the miracle of sunrise.

Why is Love so important? If it is a metaphysical ingredient of Being, why does it have to manifest itself in the world? This is a great mystery. Parmenides believes that the relationship between attraction and repulsion is a divine nexus: how it garbs itself in the world depends upon the level of consciousness within nature to manifest it as a beauty. A stone may be beautiful, but it is not always an inherent quality. A flower in full bloom definitely manifests beauty. This beauty has developed out of invisible forces of attraction and repulsion – forces that a scientist might attempt to illustrate through his understanding of enzymes, or the work of pollen-bearing stamens in flowers. An enzyme derived from sugar, for example, exfoliates to cause an extra glow in a blossom. It helps a plant to exude beauty. I can think of no better example of Love at work within our world than such an explanation. We are surrounded by it, even if we prefer to arrange our lives around the simple act of love itself.

Which leads me to consider Parmenides' understanding of Beauty. He does not mention it directly, but many of his poetic images suggest that beauty is never far from his thoughts. We must ask ourselves: why is Beauty necessary for the realization of One in the world? To answer this question we need to go elsewhere to find an answer. Plotinus, not a contemporary of Parmenides, but nonetheless a man of Pythagorean sympathies, wrote an entire tractate on Beauty in his bid to understand why it was so important.

> Beholding this Being – the Choragus [chorus leader] of all Existence, the Self-intent that ever gives forth and never takes – resting, rapt, in the vision and possession of so lofty a loveliness, growing to Its likeness, what Beauty can the Soul yet lack? For This, the Beauty supreme, the absolute and the primal, fashions Its lovers to Beauty, and makes them also worthy of love.[68]

For Plotinus there is a link between Ideal Beauty centred upon One, what he calls the 'self-intent that ever gives forth and never takes', and beauty realized in the world through the aegis of Soul. It is the first time we have come across the word 'Soul' in our exploration of One. Yet here it is, even if we place it in the context of 'soul' - that is, what we as individuals collectively possess. Soul, Plotinus tells us, transcends the sphere of

---
68   Plotinus, *Enneads*. 1.6.

things. Though devoid of mass, it is present in all mass, and possesses what he calls 'unsundered identity'. For Soul has 'never known partition', but is a 'self-gathered, integral Thing'.[69] It is this luminous essence that Beauty also possesses.

Primal Beauty is the manifestation of Soul that resides in One, with Love acting as its surrogate. Here the primordial trinity of One, Soul, and Love act in concordance. The latter two qualities are derived from One as being the 'energy' of One. Soul is the manifestation of a unity of essence in One, and similarly also as a manifestation of soul in being itself. Matter is ensouled by love, just as soul in the world is a fragment of Primal Beauty. This is how Plotinus explains it. The Ideal Form - that is, Beauty - makes its presence felt in the world as the 'sum of a harmonious coherence'. When it lights on some natural unity in a thing, it gives itself completely to that whole.[70]

Parmenides, I believe, would concur with Plotinus. Beauty is an extension of One in Being, which transforms itself into what is beautiful in being. The coherence of the whole - the ideal summation of its parts - enders beauty as a unity. The wholeness of unity applies to Soul, and so to its various functions in the world as an act of ensoulment. The philosopher Porphyry described such a process as one of *empsychia*, of the soul giving life to the composite that animates life. This idea of ensoulment lies behind Parmenides' consideration about *what is*, since it

- - - - - - - - - - - - -
69   Ibid. 4.1.
70   Ibid. 1.2.

partakes of the All Soul that inhabits One. He wants us to believe that the thing thought, and what promotes that thought, not only *is,* inseparable, but also enclosed in beauty whenever it manifests itself in the world. How else can he argue so stridently in defense of Limit? Because Limit is inherent in Beauty, and because Beauty is never diffuse, uncontained, nor unlimited.

These are just some of the issues that the *Way of Truth* evokes. It is not a poem about worldmaking, even if it intimates how that might happen. It is about how we deal with one another, as well as ourselves, in the world. When I set out to explore the poem years ago I would never have imagined that it might take me to places relating to Beauty, to Limit and Soul and the beingness of things. But it has. And it has done so as a metaphysic rather than as a crowd of ever-ostling facts playing with my rational intellect. As Wittgenstein remarked, 'I need not know all the external properties of things in the world. Instead, I must try to discover their internal properties'.[71] From Parmenides' point of view these 'internal properties' are mysteriously determined in One and are 'translated' through Being into being. We do not know why or how such an event happens, nor does Parmenides pretend to tell us.[72] All we know – and this is

• • • • • • • • • • • • •

71   Ludwig Wittgenstein, *Tractatus Logico-Philosophicus.* 2.1231.

72   Plotinus points out One extends beyond itself in a spontaneous and natural way, such as light emanating from a fire. It is a kind of 'overflowing power' stemming from unity. The Unlimited is the boundless power of One's Limit. While the Limit 'remains', the Unlimited 'proceeds'.

the miracle – it happens as an act of instantation.

The gods play with us, and we are happy that they do. Yet I ask myself: how does Parmenides' poem fit into my life now? All the years spent contemplating its meaning do at last give me a sense of familiarity. It is not that I know anythingmore about it; but One has intruded into my thoughts as more like an orange, round and full of nutriment, than as a simple, abstract sphere. The mystery of One is ever present, its stillness a pervasive influence upon how I deal with the world. The idea that Limit extends itself into Being, there to influence how I engage with the endless multiplicities that surround me, is of great comfort. Without it, I would always be casting about in the pages of some outworn theology for meaning in my life. One transcends the need to grapple with constraint as the basis for morals, or an ethic. These things are 'built in' to the numinal space which is One.

Love and Strife, those primary energies of expansion and repulsion that find their way into all of nature, where they orchestrate beauty as a 'harmonious coherence', are fitting gods to send on an errand into the realm of matter so as tostimulate at least an echo of One's unity, none other than Its luminous essence. Diastolic rhythm, as it is reflected in the dilation of the heart in order to receive blood as another form of polarizing energy, is integral to Its conduct, much as a heart muscle relaxes to allow blood to flow into its various chambers.

That One does not partake of *theos* in the old sense frees It up to act in accordance with the possibility of ensouling matter. Is it possible? As Pure Thought, that is, as thought undisturbed by the power of the imagination, One is able to ensoul matter through Its capacity to 'expand' into the universe. That It might also contract is all part of the divine dance *(theia choro)* which One enacts, in spite of the fact It is eternally unmoving.[73]

Even when I contemplate One I find myself never far from the presence of the gods, just like Parmenides.[74] His poem draws sustenance from them, and not simply as allegories. His gods are part of the act of ensoulment. They 'radiate' into being, reaching out to us as finely attuned emanations that in days past might have been visualized as nymphs, nereids, and even fairies. This is not to demean the imagination: we all need to grasp at palpable memories in the form of otherworldly presences if we are to observe the mysterious inward activity of One. Gods act in collusion with daemons, invoking their presence as nature spirits, as they still do for tribal peoples. Who are we to deny them a life? Parmenides refused to do so,

. . . .

73 In Hindu mythology Shiva is also know as *The Lord of Dance*. He is as the cosmic dancer who performs his divine dance (called Tandavam) in order to destroy a weary universe and prepare for its renewal by the god Brahma, who starts the process of creation.

74 Reminiscent of Emperor Julian Augustus, the last pagan emperor of Rome (361-63 BCE), who penned a remarkable treatise, *Hymn to the Mother of the Gods*, in defense of ancient Greek belief. In it he made a statement that echoes Parmenides' approach to writing the *Way of Truth:* 'In reality, the ancients....searched [themselves] for the cause of all eternal things... with the gods as their guides. And when they had found them, they disclosed those meanings with paradoxical myths, so that the discovery of the mythic fictions thanks to the paradoxical and the absurd, might prompt us to search for truth.'

even as he carefully crafted his metaphysical poem as a celebration of the unity of One.

The Greeks gave special credence to what they called the Unknown God (*Agnostos Theos*) to which they honoured with a temple in Athens. Perhaps this was their way of paying tribute to that inexpressible essence *(aneipoti ousia)* lying at the heart of matter, and of One. We have no way of conceiving of such an essence now that we are so wedded to the 'idea' of matter as being the sole representation of the real. Being, as in its lower case of 'being', strives towards the outside, towards a stance in *physis*. This is a long way from what the Unknown God stood for in the eyes of men like Parmenides and Socrates. If nature is to become moral, then it must transcend our need to imbue it with ordinary magical properties. Parmenides' One helps us to make such a transition. It is the embodiment of unity, which in itself is of a high moral order.

A goddess that Parmenides did not mention in his poem was Pistis. As one of the Charities, she enabled men to reach beyond the habitude of their critical faculties and gaze upon the world without prejudice. Trust is a quality that weno longer rely upon to the extent that the Greeks might have. I ask myself why. While Parmenides' poem is firmly grounded in a metaphysic more than in knowledge as a condition of being, nonetheless one feels he relies on Trust to help him in his endeavor. One embodies Trust as well as Limit. It is almost as if he had to learn how to trust in where his logic might ultimately lead. Towards determinism or towards the open space of a finite, self-creating universe? I believe the answer lies in the latter: of a moving outwards of One into Being, even while it remains unmoving at its centre. Should we not trust in the seemingly random nature of multiplicity, even though we know it to be an illusion? Parmenides tells us that we must. Negation is the first transition from nothing into something.

Do I acknowledge Trust in my own life? After contemplating the *Way of Truth* all these years, I am nearer to doing so. The innate stability of One fills me with trust. I see It now as I might the Unknown God occupying a place in my life that previously would have been reserved for the act of calculation and control, of my allegiance to *physis*. Trust frees me from the constraints of such manipulatory acts. For all its inner reserve, One is an ever-giving entity that relies upon my ability to trust. Where unity prevails, so does trust. It is the 'awesome Prior' that Plotinus views as the primary concept of unity.[75] As he say, 'That awesome Prior, the Unity, is not a being, for so its unity would be vested in something else.'

I begin to view the universe as one vast poem whose language is neither elegiac nor lyrical. Trust underpins its existence, a motionless act of giving that goes on and on, star after star, so that their myriad brightnesses culminate in the ease of unknowing. Why? Because they illumine *(ellampei to theion phos)* the absolute and unending dimension of the universe. For trust is about not knowing, nor caring too much. It is about reaching out and taking the

---

75   Plotinus, *Enneads.* 6.9.5.

hand of a goddess whenever it is offered.

I no longer see this Mistress as the Queen of the Underworld. She no longer inhabits the darker places of my unconscious, febrile and illusive always, where she has spent an age tinkering with my selfhood, making me feel uneasy. But Parmenides, through the advent of his great poem, has allowed me to drive my own chariot towards her through cloud-lined gates, there to take her hand in mine. The Goddess is now my companion on the way of *what is*, no more taunting me with her seductive demeanor as in the old days.

I am nearing the end of my journey. Parmenides' great poem has yielded so much gold dust. A master metaphysician, the philosopher has found a way to assuage all my concerns about the relationship between Being and being. In the past I would have seen these as formidable hurdles to jump over in my quest to understand the nature of Primary Substance *(Kyria Ousia)*. To my mind One is a beautiful expression of that condition. For all their great work in cosmology by modern astrophysicists and scientists, names such as the 'big bang' or 'dark matter' do not have the power to stimulate my thoughts as does One, the primary substance of Being.

That Parmenides rendered One as a sphere helps me to understand this complex and never-ending mystery at the heart of life. I want to touch it, I want to hold it, but I know I cannot. At least Parmenides has given me a taste for its finely rendered contradiction as a premise for all existence. As Plato was to write in defense of Parmenides fundamental insight: 'If there is a One, the One is both all things and nothing whatsoever.'[76] Such a perfect paradox. I can live with it because I now know that it is protected by a god, by Pistis. One simply *has* to exist.

What is, Parmenides tells me, being one and homogenous, is indivisible. No more can I escape this fact. I can pretend that *what isn't* is a good place to be whenever I live and enjoy the surface play of life, but I know ultimately that this is not the right path to follow. Why? Having learnt how to trust in the contradictory nature of *what is* as a genuine pathway to truth, I find myself living in a state of simple acceptance of the fact that, as Aristotle relates, the divine encloses the whole of nature.[77] He further states that some things do not go away simply because they are divinely inspired *(theopnefstos)*. At Parmenides' urging, I am happy to accept nature and the world as being imbued with the divine.

Am I so far away from my ancient inheritance? Not really, at least not now. During the course of writing this book I have come to know Parmenides less as an enigmatic person, to whom nonetheless I felt a strange attraction, than a man whose capacity as an *ouliades,* as a healer, still had the power to invigorate my soul whenever I felt something amiss. His great poem still touches me with its message. It goes to the heart of things, and represents a flight of quintessential importance.

• • • • • • • • • • • • •

76   Plato, *Parmenides.* 160B.

77   Aristotle, *Metaphysics.* A8, 1074b 1. Also, Thales, when he says 'Water is pervaded by a divine power capable of moving it.'

I reminded myself that Shakespeare asked the same question as he did 2,000 year later, not recognizing that Parmenides had already answered it. For the playwright, 'to be or not to be' was a conundrum; whereas for the philosopher it was the paradox that constituted being itself. Not for one moment did Parmenides live in the shadow of Hamlet's existential angst. Because he knew, as Hamlet did not, that the visible world is its own myth, a tale half true and half false, a truth that is One.

Finally I re-enter the world with a new feeling of confidence. Parmenides has taught me how to live. An ancient Greek philosopher has reached out to me across time to deliver his message. At the onset of this journey I would not have believed possible such an enduring prospect. His words are no longer a footnote to Greek philosophy any more. His poem has entered the pantheon of seminal texts that have changed how we view the world. Along with the Gospels, Upanishads, and Tao Te Ching, it has become both a cultural artifact as well as a call to action in thought. When Parmenides tells me that *it is* can never be confused with not-being, I am reminded of Laozi's remark in his ancient Chinese commentary, published in the sixth-century BCE, which sounds so similar to that of the philosopher's: 'The Tao that can be told is not the eternal Tao. The name that can be named is not the eternal name.' Parmenides and Laozi were almost contemporaries, and came up with similar ideas. Perhaps they both derived their unique knowledge of the Way (Tao) from the same source.

It remains to be seen if these reflections have made Parmenides more pertinent to our age. I take into account that great poets do disappear from our thoughts from time to time, there to await revival by a new generation. It is hard to know whether delving into the *Way of Truth* and exploring its philosophic implications are any more relevant today. We live in an age where *physis* reigns supreme, a bulwark upon which we stand gazing into the future with not a little trepidation. The old certainties have fallen into abeyance, even as we glory in testing nature to is limits – and, I might add, at a considerable cost. I can't help feeling that Parmenides' poem tells us something important about Limit, and about ourselves. We need to listen to what he has to say, knowing that we live in a finite and precious universe. Limit, I now believe, is the source of all beauty, and all hope.

Afterword

Ancient Greek philosophy urges us to think in a primordial way. It is a thinking based upon the rigorous use of logic; but it does on occasion enter the otherworldly domain of pure metaphysics when logic finally reaches its apex, a place from which it can no longer further ascend. We are not so familiar with how to make such a transition because we are accustomed to thinking materially. Such a way of thinking is firmly based upon the demands of *physis*. Modern science and economics inhabit this domain; they never stray far from what can be measured or calculated. It is this world, the world of *techne*, that men like Parmenides ask us to put aside if ever we wish to think metaphysically. How does one think metaphysically? It is the most enduring question and challenge of our time. To break with our dependence upon *techne*, to question the integrity of things as things, is to ask us to re-align our thinking towards a uni-dimensional world where contrariety and paradox come into their own. This is what philosophers such as Parmenides teach us. The ramifications of his revolutionary insights echo down through the ages – through Plato, Plotinus, Saint Augustine, Dionysius the Areopagite, John Scotus Erugena, and on into the thought of such modern thinkers as Novalis and Martin Heidegger, to name just a few not aligned to a fixation with scientific enquiry.[78] If we but admit it to ourselves, the deep stream of Parmenides' thought flows through to us even today.

Parmenides did not address the issues of time or duration to the extent that he might have, or could, in his poem, *Way of Truth*. But he sounded the opening bars to a remarkable piece of music, music that we still faintly hear two-and-half thousand years later. We live our lives in time, yet we continue to perceive of a condition that stands outside time - none other than an eternal condition. Somehow we sense, beyond what logic will ever teach us, that we also live non-temporal lives, even as we age and our bodies begin to fail us. This is not such a bad thing, merely an acknowledgement that in spite of everything a part of us shares the realm of the gods, and another part does not.

We have the possibility if we are truthful with ourselves to become half-gods, what the Greeks regarded as a state of *hemitheos*, as mentioned earlier. Many of their heroes were considered to be half-gods, people such as Achilles, Helen, and Hercules, for example. Holderlin,

---

[78] Albert Einstein, for example, often saw his theories as a product of Parmenidean thought.(Popper)

that great eighteenth-century German poet, alluded to it when he wrote: 'I grew up in the arms of gods.' It is not really so unnatural for us to want to attain to a state of *hemitheos* in this life, even if we find it difficult to do so.

We need to make the decision that it is a worthwhile endeavor. If One is able to inhale the void and exhale a fully formed universe as some ancient philosophers tell us (speaking metaphysically), is it not possible for us to find a way to make primordial thinking a part of the very fabric of our lives once more, just as they did? To do so would be to introduce a measure of risk and uncertainty into how we view the underlying principles that constitute the universe. Parmenides tells us that One overarches Being and, as a consequence, being-in-the-world. As remote as it is, One is nonetheless every-present in everything that constitutes being and its physical composition, including change, diminution, and renewal. Such is the miracle of One: it has the power to be All in all while never actually being present.

One appears to us in a multitude of forms, and distinguishes itself in myriads of ways. The beauty of the world is a mark of One's capacity to outflow into being. The sidelong glance of a deer in the wild as it contemplates flight from danger is a manifestation of One. One gives us our capacity for circumspection so that we are able to perceive things purely and simply as objects existing in the moment. Nor do we perform such acts merely because we have eyes or ears. We do so because, when our entire being rests in a state of wholeness, we find ourselves able to live through the pleasure of memory-driven experience.

One helps us to attain to foreknowledge, what the Greeks call *phronesis*. A piece of coral possesses it when the moment arises each year to spawn, so that conception might begin across the warm waters of a reef like a cloudburst. In this way One reveals to us the measure of its capacity for All or Nothing, not as a fulfillment of the void, but of the incomplete. Conception is a demonstration of Limit giving way to the Unlimited, of *peras* precipitating *apeiron*. As a consequence One is nothing other than Itself. It always *is*, atemporal and complete, a deep-breathing absence that forever holds us in its arms.

It is important to emphasize that Parmenides' One is not unreachable. All he wished to announce was that it is not a substance in the ordinary sense of the word, nor is it a god. He wants us to understand that only in metaphysics could a non-substantial One occupy a non-space that is always in close proximity to us. One is not material, and yet it pre-exists and determines what is material. Call it a paradox, and accept that such paradoxes do exist in the mind of One – that is, if One possesses a mind, which it does not! Primordial opposites do have a place in the heart of Being, however, whereby they can play out in being, in our own lives too, as the driving force of existence. To turn one's back on One, as Parmenides tells us when we embroil ourselves in what *is not*, is to accept the illusion of life as an absolute, which it is not.

The beauty of One is that it can only be approached through intuitive intellection. It cannot be analyzed, nor can It possess any real form except by way of the image offered to us by Parmenides when he described It as a sphere. Beyond this image we cannot venture. We might want something more substantial, given our love of what is palpable, but finally we must accept that this is not possible. One defies all attempts to corral it as a sensible object. We can only know of One through Its emanations as a multiplicity, a *plethos* acting out the realization of the world. Where It fulfills all our expectations is when Love presents itself as a striving towards unity in the domain of *plethos* itself. Love is Its messenger, Its unifier, Its pressing back of discord and strife that fill our everyday lives. Suffering becomes Its succor and balm as we strive to overcome Neikos, the god of anguish and hate.

Sometimes I am at a loss to know how to fulfill my own obligation towards One. How do I express the sheer wonder and awe that I feel at observing the vast interstellar space that is the universe, of which I am but an infinitesimal part? How do I accommodate and accept the tectonic forces of suffering that enshroud humanity as an expression of Neikos doing battle with Philia? Strife seems so paramount in this grave hour. Will Love again overcome? I take comfort in the knowledge that Parmenides would have known that, truly, nothing can be done to modify the play of cosmic events as they happen. One's capacity for showering forth destruction is a powerful reminder that we do not have the capacity to change the way the world works. We are Its unlikely playthings, ensouled as we are by One's delight in confabulating the reality of our being. Joy is Its gift.

To give Parmenides his due, he did not set out to write a practical guide to life. This was not his aim. Rather, he wanted to point out that in order to arrive at a correct way of living, one has to understand the nature of falsity and illusion as a veiled entity living behind the assumptions of *physis*. The world of appearance is not a viable basis for a life lived in truth. This is a condition of what *is not* – and not-being is its figment. To live a life in truth one must always contemplate Being as an invisible agency of One. Truth lies in understanding the full ramification of unity, not in the power to discriminate or hold opinions. These are aspects of duality, of determination, and of prejudice only. A person who lives in full collusion with One and with unity is always going to be someone who understands the power of Limit to frame his or her life.

Parmenides represents our future, not our past. We need to come to terms with One as a supreme metaphysical reality once more. To do so, we must find a way back to primordial thinking, to a thinking that always remains close to the sheer wonder of being alive, rather than a thinking that aligns itself with process. Such thinking is the thinking of what *is not*. How we do so becomes an individual thing: one has to assess our own life predicament, find out what our limits are, and live according to their injunctions. One embodies care. To be seized by care as that of a cossetting, a cradling, is to know that all is right with the world, even if one's personal circumstance suggests otherwise.[79]

We are living in an age of significant human conflict. But then, so did Parmenides: his family quit Ionia in the wake of invasion and political instability. Yet after he had attained to adulthood he did not use exile as an excuse for feeling disappointed with his lot. Rather, he befriended Ameinias, a man said to be of no note or position in society, except that of being a sage. From him he learnt how to think – of number and musical theory, of limit, unity and plurality, and of 'even-oddness' *(artiperossis)* as a constituent of Being, which he later turned into one of the most important concepts in philosophy.[80] One is the high point upon which we now stand, thanks to him. He revealed to us that Truth can only be found in cultivating our inward glance towards Being.

- - - - - - - - - - - - - -

[79] We are reminded of Athena's undoubted concern for Diomedes when she came to his aid in the midst of battle outside Troy's walls, as depicted in *The Iliad*: 'Even such a flame did she kindle from his head and shoulders; and she sent him into the midst where men thronged the thickest.' (Bk 5, 1-8)

[80] According to Theon of Smyrna, Aristotle maintained that One partakes of both natures, even-oddness or *artiperissos*, because One when added to an even number becomes odd, but if it is added to an odd number it makes it even. Pythagoras apparently taught such a number-system as the basis of the physical universe. This concept lies at the heart of Parmenides' understanding of One. We must bear in mind that the number-system is metaphysical rather than mathematical.

A world in a state of disjunction is merely an expression of the timeless maledictions of strife. Strife is umbilically linked to Love, each urging the other out of its inertia and passivity. They are the primary forces of Being which foliate in being by way of their particular activities. We need to understand this tug-of-war for what it is: a rebalancing of the forces of nature, both physical and psychological, that lie at the root of existence. By Its nature One husbands unity as an overarching panacea when all seems lost. We need to remember that being out of kilter is sometimes a good thing: it helps us to recognize that we have strayed too far from our limits. We must also recognize that straying *from* our limits on occasions is a generative act. The trick is to know when to pull back.

Parmenides is a great teacher. He has taught us how to think metaphysically, and to cultivate a state of *metaphysis*. Nor are myth and religion an important part of his armory, though he does allude to them. We should be grateful that he has freed our minds to think in a more transcendent way, untrammelled by the constraints of the epic tradition or theology. It is to dance on a broader stage. I can't help believing that if he were alive today Parmenides would ask us to return to the basics. Don't rush into divertissements or up blind alleys. Don't try to tear matter apart in a bid to unlock its mysteries for the sake of knowledge only. Remember that One is a mystery which should not be tampered with for the sake of indulging in endless and unnecessary discoveries, however much they are capable of being justified. We must remember also that a Faustian bargain is never easy to unravel once made.

Let us be thankful that Parmenides did appear over our horizon. Some might argue that his *Way of Truth* is merely a repost to Pythagorean arguments about number and the void then very much in vogue in southern Italy. I detect no animosity towards any of his predecessors in his poem, however. Rather, I sensea man in league with a revelation too great to bear alone. He needed to let others know of what he had discovered. The concept of One had come to rest in him like an eagle in its eyrie. Its talons clasped him to its breast. In knowingwhat he did he had become not only a master poet, but a *hemitheos* in the tradition of other men blessed by the gods. He had entered upon the Way of Truth where men of a certain note know themselves to have become more than who they are. I am reminded of Plotinus' remarks to this effect:

> There are two stages of the journey for all, one when they are going up andone when they have arrived above. The first leads from the regions below, the second is for those who are already in the intelligible realm and have gained their footing there.[81]

Living in the intelligible world became second nature to Parmenides. In doing so, his loftiness as a poet and metaphysician transformed the way we think about our universe, and made it accessible to us through

---

81 *Ennead* I. 3 [20] 1. 13.

the miraculous and incomprehensible nature of One. We should acknowledge that he alone had the courage to climb that slope – and, at the same time, clear a pathway for us to follow in his footsteps.

His greatest contribution to our lives today is in the knowledge that in order to live a full and fruitful life we must recognize in everything we say and do a distinction between accepting the aeternality and isness of One as its governing factor, and not the not-being or non-reality of the physical world, which is illusory at best. In doing so, we then begin to understand the limitations of being-in-the-world as a true reality. This is not to say that any attempt to deny the value of our lives in the world is valid – far from it. What Parmenides wants us to accept is that there are two worlds, even though one of them cannot be considered real: the world of pure metaphysics and that of *physis*. By accepting One and Being as the supreme exemplar of unity *(peras)* we open ourselves upto a more elevated sense of who we are – to a life that is more spirituallyrealized and whole.

He is alerting us to the paradoxical fact that Being *does not exist* as such, because it has no past or future, because it does not partake of time at all. When we understand this fact, fully and without reserve, then we begin to comprehend the extraordinary nature of One, of oneness itself. In the greatscheme of things identity and difference have no reality any more; they are simply our way of attaching ourselves to the illusion of existence as a way of living in the world.

Nor does Parmenides not want us to live in the world; he is not asking us to turn our back upon it. All he is asking us to do is to recognize that unity, the absolute completeness of Being *(oulomeles),* is of far greater importance to our inner wellbeing and health than any perceived sense of security that we might wish to achieve through our daily life activity. Preserving our place in the world as individuals is of less importance than in learning how to celebrate the awful glory of One. Only this can be defined as the Way of Truth.

FINIS

Appendix 1

In a little-known book by a fifth century Roman physician, Caelius Aurelianus, we find an explanation of Fragment 17 of Parmenides' poem, in his *Tardarum Passionum*. Caeleus tells us of what is known as the doctrine of the 'double seed' as it is derived from Parmenides. It refers to a complex understanding of how children are conceived, and its effects on character after birth:

> When semen flows from the right testicle, settles and grows in the right side of the uterus, boys resembling their father are born. When the fluid flows from the left testicle, and settles and grows in the right side of the uterus, boys resembling their mother are born. When semen settles and grows in the left side of the uterus, girls will result – and presumably from semen of the right testicle girls resembling their father, and from semen of the left testicle girls resembling their mother.
> When the seed which comes from the right testicle and flows to the left part of the uterus, or that which

comes from the left testicle to the right side of the uterus, this produce unity, to which the process we read in Parmenides' fragment then applies.

In one case, a boy (sexually male) with feminine characteristics (ie. like his mother to a greater or lesser degree) is born, and in the other a girl with masculine characteristics is born. One must assume in such a case thatwhen the semen of the right testicle flows to the right side of the uterus, or that of the left side goes to the left of the uterus, the seeds never fail to produce unity. When the seed goes to the contrary side of the uterus, it may happen that the seeds from testicle and uterus fail to produce a unity, and a child tormented by double seed is born.[82]

This complex argument informs us of how ancient medical practitioners accounted for individual difference in children born of the same parents. It gives us some insight into the reasons why some children grow up to become tormented souls, and others to enjoy a more balanced and happy life. It also accounts for the confusing nature of Fragment 17 as it is rendered in the poem, *Way of Truth* because it does not have any clear meaning unless an interpolation is added:

[In the uterus] on the right males and females on the left...

- - - - - - - - - - - - - -
82   Translated by Leonardo Tarán, *Parmenides*.

Select Bibliography

Armstrong, A. H. *The Architecture of the Intelligible Universe in the Philosophy of Plotinus*. (London: Cambridge University Press, 1940)

Barnes, Jonathan (Transl.) *Early Greek Philosophy*. (London: PenguinClassics, 1987)

Burnet, John. *Early Greek Philosophy*. (London: Adam & Charles Black, 1948)
- *Greek Philosophy* (London: Macmillan and Co., 1928)

Cornford, F. M. *Greek Religious Thought from Homer to the Age of Alexander*. (London: J. M. Dent & Co.)
- *Plato and Parmenides* (London: Routledge & Kegan Paul, 1951)
- *From Philosophy to Religion*. (New York: Dover Books, 2004)

Crudden, Michael (Transl.) *The Homeric Hymns*. (Oxford: Oxford University Press, 2001)

Curd, Patricia. *The Legacy of Parmenides*. Las Vegas: Parmenides Publishing, 2005)

Dodds, E. R. *Selected Passages Illustrating Neoplatonism*. (London: Society for Promotion of Christian Knowledge, 1923)
- *The Greeks and the Irrational* (Berkley: University of CaliforniaPress, 1951)

Gallop, David, *Parmenides of Elea*. Toronto: University of Toronto Press,2016)

Hadot, Pierre. *Plotinus*. (Chicago: the University of Chicago Press, 1998)
- *Philosophy as a Way of Life*. (Oxford: Blackwood Publishers, 1995)
- *What is Ancient Philosophy?* (Cambridge Mass.: HarvardUniversity Press, 2002)

Heath, Sir Thomas L. *Greek Astronomy*. (New York: Dover Publications, 1991)

Heidegger, Martin. *Parmenides*. (Bloomington: Indiana Press, 1996)

Homer. *The Iliad*. (Transl. Robert Fitzgerald) (London: Everyman's Library,1992)

Iamblicus. *The Life of Pythagoras*. Transl. Thomas Taylor, 1821. (Hollywood:Theosophical Publishing House, 1918)

Jaeger, Werner. *The Theology of the Early Greek Philosophers*. (Oxford: OxfordUniversity Press, 1967)

Kahn, Charles h. *The Art and Thought of Heraclitus*. (Cambridge: CambridgeUniversity Press, 1995)

Kingsley, Peter. *In the Dark Places of Wisdom*. (Point Reyes: The Golden Sufi Centre, 1999)

Lattimore, Richard. (Tansl.) *The Odes of Pindar*. (Chicago: The University ofChicago, 1969)

Lombardo, Stanley. (Transl.) *Parmenides and Empedocles*. (San Francisco:Grey Fox Press)

Mascaro, Juan. *The Upanishads*. (London: Penguin Books, 1965)

MacKenna, Stephen (Transl.) *Plotinus, the Enneads*. (London: Faber and FaberLimited, 1969)

Murray, Gilbert. *Five Stages of Greek Religion*. (Westport: Greenwood Press,1976)

Nahm, Milton. *Selections from Early Greek Philosophy.* (New York: F.S. Crofts& Co. 1940)

Neitzsche, Friedrich. *Philosophy in the Tragic Age of the Greeks.* (WashingtonDC: Gateway Press, 1962)

Otto, Walter F. *The Homeric Gods.* (London: Thames & Hudson, 1969)

Popper, Karl R. *The World of Parmenides.* (London: Routledge, 1998)

Plato. *The Collected Dialogues of Plato.* Edit. Edith Hamilton. (Princeton: Princeton University Press)

Philip, J. H. *Pythagoras and Early Pythagoreanism.* (Toronto: University ofToronto Press, 1968)

Remes, Pauliina. *Neoplatonism.* (Berkley: University of California Press, 2008)

Siorvanes, Lucas. *Proclus, Neo-Platonic Philosophy and Science.* (Edinburgh: Edinburgh University Press, 1996)

Tarán, Leonardo. *Parmenides.* (Princeton: Princeton University Press, 1965)

Thomas, Rosalind. *Literacy and Orality in Ancient Greece.* (London: Cambridge University Press, 1999)

Schelling, Friedrich, *The Ages of the World.* (New York: Columbia University Press, 1942)

Slaveva-Griffin, Svetla. *Plotinus on Number.* (Oxford: Oxford University Press, 2009)

Wallis, R. T. *Neoplatonism.* (New York: Charles Scribner's Sons, 1972)

West, M.L. *Early Greek Philosophy and the Orient.* (London: Oxford University Press, 1971)

PARMENIDES' CONCEPT

OF ONE

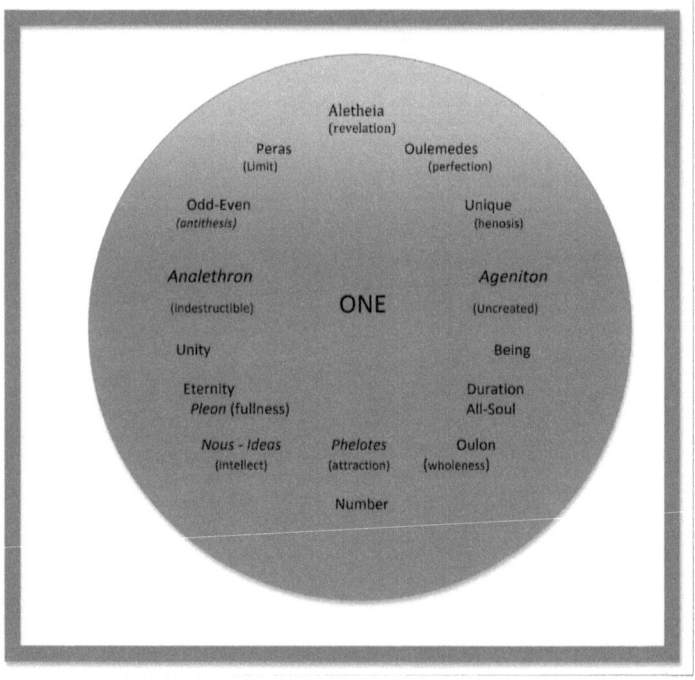

CONCEPT OF ONE

IN RELATION TO WORLD APPEARANCE

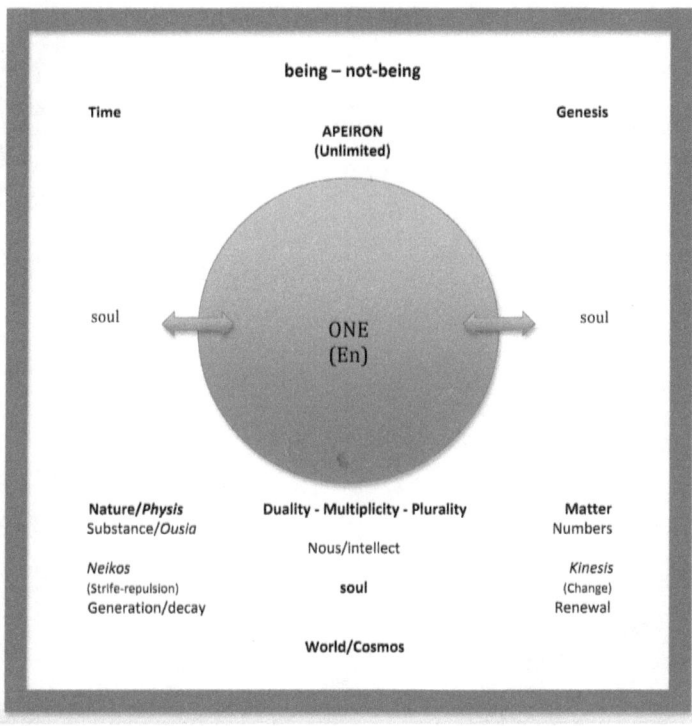